THE
CONSTITUTION
Past, Present, and Future

Revised Edition

HOLT, RINEHART AND WINSTON
Harcourt Brace & Company
Austin • New York • Orlando • Atlanta • San Francisco • Boston • Dallas • Toronto • London

Printed in the United States of America

ISBN 0-03-050782-0
   6 021 00

CONTENTS

THE CONSTITUTION:
PAST, PRESENT, AND FUTURE

Imagine that you and your classmates are magically transported to a place where no one has ever lived before. Imagine that you are the only people living in this place. There are enough plants, animals, and water for you to have food, clothing, and shelter. What else would you need? Would you need a government?

The English philosopher John Locke described this situation as a state of nature. And he said that in a state of nature, there existed natural laws. These laws said that no one must harm other people or take away their property or their happiness. Locke said that no government would exist to protect those rights until one was formed. But in order for a government to be formed, the people had to consent, or agree, to be governed. This philosophy was a powerful influence on our leaders and is expressed in the Declaration of Independence and the Constitution.

But our form of government did not begin with the Constitution. It did not start with the Revolutionary War or even with the first colonists. The people who settled our country had brought with them strong ideas about government and the protection of the basic rights of people.

In 1215 King John of England was forced to sign the Magna Carta, which said that the king was not allowed to take away the rights of the nobles. Although the Magna Carta applied only to the upper classes, it was an important step in limiting the power of the kings. More importantly, the Magna Carta inspired in people the desire to extend the rights that it promised. (For the full text of the Magna Carta, see the Appendix, page 109.)

The Magna Carta is a written compact, or agreement. As far back as biblical times, people were making compacts, or covenants. Such religious compacts had great influence on government. When the Pilgrims sailed for America in 1620, they prepared a plan of government. The plan they drew up was similar to a religious compact. This compact was a social compact, and the purpose was to make laws for the general good of the people. Because the ship the Pilgrims were sailing on was called the *Mayflower*, they called their compact the Mayflower Compact. (For the full text of the Mayflower Compact, see the Appendix, page 119.)

Although the first colonists were under English rule, England was far away and could not always watch over the colonies. The colonists needed some form of local government. When problems arose, the residents gathered to settle them. In these town meetings everyone had an opportunity to voice his or her opinion and to vote. But as the number of colonists grew and the settlements spread out across the countryside, it became harder and harder to call everyone together in a town meeting. So, colonial Americans created governments much like the English government that was their heritage.

The settlers who came to America from England brought with them a tradition of representative government. A representative government is one in which a small group of people speaks for a large group of people. Usually the representatives are elected by the people. The idea of a representative government had started in England with the establishment of Parliament in 1258. Parliament was an assembly of people who made laws and limited the power of the king. For example, the king could not tax the people unless

Parliament agreed. You can read the limits that Parliament put on the king in a document called the English Bill of Rights, written in 1689. (For the full text of the English Bill of Rights, see the Appendix, page 115.)

The first representative government in the colonies was an assembly, or group of people, elected by the property owners of Virginia in 1619. The members of the assembly called themselves "Burgesses." They borrowed this word from England. Originally, it meant a member of Parliament who represented a borough (town) or a university. Virginia's House of Burgesses was the first body of lawmakers to be elected in the English colonies. After Parliament passed the English Bill of Rights in 1689, it insisted that all of the English colonies have representative governments.

The colonists had a great deal of freedom to govern themselves. In 1776 the colonists voted to break free of English rule and had to fight a war to gain their independence. The Continental Congress drew up a document called the Articles of Confederation to govern the newly independent states. The Articles created a confederation, or association, among the 13 states. The states were given many powers of self-government. The Articles also created a central government, but it did not have very much power. It did not have the authority to settle squabbles among the states. Congress did not have the power to collect taxes. There was no president to enforce the acts of Congress. There was no national court system. The weakness of the central government caused many problems.

To solve the problems that the new nation was facing, in 1787 the Continental Congress called a meeting to revise the Articles of Confederation. But instead of revising the Articles, the delegates to this convention created a new document, the Constitution of the United States.

The Constitution embodies the strong tradition of democratic government that Americans had developed. Many of the framers of the Constitution were scholars who studied the works of great philosophers and historians. They were guided by the spirit of democracy and set out to create a plan of government that protected that tradition. But the writers of the Constitution did not always agree on how best to accomplish that end, so the document contains many compromises. The document they created, the Constitution of the United States, is one of the greatest documents ever written. It provides an outline for government. But its framers built in an amazing flexibility. It is this flexibility that has helped our Constitution stand strong for more than 200 years.

The Constitution of the United States

The following text of the United States Constitution reflects the original spelling and usage. Brackets [ ] indicate parts that have been changed or set aside by amendments. Additional paragraphs printed in a different typeface are not part of the Constitution. They explain the meaning of certain passages, or they describe how certain passages have worked in practice.

PREAMBLE

We the People of the United States, in Order to form a more perfect Union, establish Justice, insure domestic Tranquility, provide for the common defence, promote the general Welfare, and secure the Blessings of Liberty to ourselves and our Posterity, do ordain and establish this Constitution for the United States of America.

ARTICLE I
The Legislative Branch

Section 1

All legislative Powers herein granted shall be vested in a Congress of the United States, which shall consist of a Senate and House of Representatives.

The first three articles of the Constitution divide the powers of the United States government among three separate branches: (1) the legislative branch, represented by Congress; (2) the executive branch, represented by the president; and (3) the judicial branch, represented by

the Supreme Court. This division, called the *separation of powers,* is designed to prevent any branch of the government from becoming too powerful.

Article I says that only Congress has the power to make laws. Congress cannot give these powers to any other body. Through the years, however, Congress has created various federal agencies to make regulations and put its policies into practice. Such agencies include the Federal Trade Commission, the Consumer Product Safety Commission, and the Interstate Commerce Commission.

The two-house Congress was one of the most important compromises of the Constitutional Convention. The small states at the Convention supported the *New Jersey Plan,* under which each state would have had the same number of representatives. The large states wanted the *Virginia Plan,* which provided representation based on population. As a compromise, one house was chosen according to each plan.

Section 2

The House of Representatives

(1) The House of Representatives shall be composed of Members chosen every second Year by the People of the several States, and the Electors in each State shall have the Qualifications requisite for Electors of the most numerous Branch of the State Legislature.

Members of the House of Representatives are elected to two-year terms. If a person is eligible to vote for the "most numerous branch" of his or her state legislature, he or she is also eligible to vote for members of Congress. The "most numerous branch" is the house with the most members. All states except Nebraska have a two-house state legislature. The question of who can vote for state legislators is entirely up to the state, subject to the restrictions of the Constitution and federal law, such as the Voting Rights Act of 1965. The 15th, 19th, 24th, and 26th Amendments forbid the states to deny or restrict a citizen's right to vote because of race, sex, or failure to pay a tax; or because of age if the person is at least 18 years old.

(2) No Person shall be a Representative who shall not have attained to the Age of twenty five Years, and been seven Years a Citizen of the United States, and who shall not, when elected, be an Inhabitant of that State in which he shall be chosen.

Each state decides for itself the requirements for legal residence, subject to constitutional limits. Most representatives live not only in the state but also in the district from which they are chosen.

(3) Representatives and direct Taxes shall be apportioned among the several States which may be included within this Union, according to their respective Numbers, [which shall be determined by adding to the whole Number of free Persons, including those bound to Service for a Term of Years, and excluding Indians not taxed, three fifths of all other Persons.] The actual Enumeration shall be made within three Years after the first Meeting of the Congress of the United States, and within every subsequent Term of ten Years, in such Manner as they shall by Law direct. The number of Representatives shall not exceed one for every thirty Thousand, but each State shall have at Least one Representative; [and until such enumeration shall be made, the State of New Hampshire shall be entitled to chuse three, Massachusetts eight, Rhode Island and Providence Plantations one, Connecticut five, New-York six, New Jersey four, Pennsylvania eight, Delaware one, Maryland six, Virginia ten, North Carolina five, South Carolina five, and Georgia three.]

The effect of this paragraph has been greatly changed, both by amendments and by new conditions. It now provides only three things: (1) the number of representatives given to each state shall be based on its population; (2) Congress must see that the people of the United States are counted every 10 years; and (3) each state gets at least one representative.

The words "and direct taxes" mean poll and property taxes. The 16th Amendment gives Congress the right to tax a person according to the size of his or her income, rather than according to the population of the state in which the person lives. The phrase still forbids Congress to collect any form of direct taxation except by dividing it among the states according to population.

In the reference to "three fifths of all other Persons," the "other Persons" meant African American slaves. Since there are no longer any slaves, this part of the paragraph no longer has any meaning.

The requirement that there shall be no more than one representative for every 30,000 persons no longer has practical force. There is now one representative for about every 519,000 persons. In 1929 Congress fixed the total number of representatives at 435.

(4) When vacancies happen in the Representation from any State, the Executive Authority thereof shall issue Writs of Election to fill such Vacancies.

If a vacancy occurs in a House seat, the state governor must call a special election to fill it. However, if the next regularly scheduled election is to be held soon, the governor may allow the seat to remain empty rather than call a special election.

(5) The House of Representatives shall chuse their Speaker and other Officers; and shall have the sole Power of Impeachment.

The House chooses an officer called the *Speaker* to lead meetings. The House alone has the power to bring impeachment charges against an official. The Senate tries impeachment cases.

Section 3

The Senate

(1) The Senate of the United States shall be composed of two Senators from each State, [chosen by the Legislature thereof,] for six Years; and each Senator shall have one Vote.

The Constitution at first provided that each state legislature should select the state's two senators. The 17th Amendment, ratified in 1913, changed this provision by allowing the voters of each state to choose their own senators.

(2) Immediately after they shall be assembled in Consequence of the first Election, they shall be divided as equally as may be into three Classes. The Seats of the Senators of the first Class shall be vacated at the Expiration of the second Year, of the second Class at the Expiration of the fourth Year, and of the third Class at the Expiration of the sixth Year, so that one third may be chosen every second Year; [and if Vacancies happen by Resignation, or otherwise, during the Recess of the Legislature of any State, the Executive thereof may make temporary Appointments until the next Meeting of the Legislature, which shall then fill such Vacancies.]

Senators are elected to six-year terms. Every two years, one-third of the senators are elected and two-thirds are holdovers. This arrangement makes the Senate a continuing body, unlike the House, whose entire membership is elected every two years. The 17th Amendment changed the method of filling vacancies. The governor chooses a senator until the people elect one.

(3) No Person shall be a Senator who shall not have attained to the Age of thirty Years, and been nine Years a Citizen of the United States, and who shall not, when elected, be an Inhabitant of that State for which he shall be chosen.

In 1806 Henry Clay of Kentucky was appointed to fill an unexpired term in the Senate. He was only 29, a few months younger than the minimum age, but no one challenged the appointment. In 1793 Albert Gallatin was elected to the Senate from Pennsylvania. He was barred from taking office because he had not been a citizen for nine years.

(4) The Vice President of the United States shall be President of the Senate, but shall have no Vote, unless they be equally divided.

The vice president serves as president of the Senate but votes only when a tie vote occurs. The vice president's power to break ties can be important. In 1789, for example, Vice President John Adams cast the vote that decided the pres-

ident could remove cabinet members without Senate approval.

(5) The Senate shall chuse their other Officers, and also a President pro tempore, in the Absence of the Vice President, or when he shall exercise the Office of President of the United States.

The Senate elects an officer called the *president pro tempore* to lead meetings when the vice president is absent.

(6) The Senate shall have the sole Power to try all Impeachments. When sitting for that Purpose, they shall be on Oath or Affirmation. When the President of the United States is tried, the Chief Justice shall preside: And no Person shall be convicted without the Concurrence of two thirds of the Members present.

The provision that the chief justice, rather than the vice president, shall preside over the Senate when a president is on trial probably grows out of the fact that a conviction would make the vice president the president. The phrase "on Oath or Affirmation" means that senators are placed under oath when trying impeachment cases, just as jurors are in a regular court trial.

(7) Judgment in Cases of Impeachment shall not extend further than to removal from Office, and disqualification to hold and enjoy any Office of honor, Trust or Profit under the United States: but the Party convicted shall nevertheless be liable and subject to Indictment, Trial, Judgment and Punishment, according to Law.

If an impeached person is found guilty, he or she can be removed from office and forbidden to hold federal office again. The Senate cannot impose any other punishment, but the person may also be tried in regular courts. The Senate has convicted only five persons, all of them judges. These judges were removed from office, but only one was tried in another court.

Section 4

Organization of Congress

(1) The Times, Places and Manner of holding Elections for Senators and Representatives, shall be described in each State by the Legislature thereof; but the Congress may at any time by Law make or alter such Regulations, [except as to the places of chusing Senators.]

As long as state legislatures chose the senators, it would not do to let Congress fix the place of choosing. This allowance would have amounted to giving Congress the power to tell each state where to locate its capital. The words "except as to the Places of chusing Senators" were set aside by the 17th Amendment.

(2) The Congress shall assemble at least once in every Year, [and such Meeting shall be on the first Monday in December,] unless they shall by Law appoint a different Day.

In Europe monarchs could keep parliaments from meeting, sometimes for many years, simply by not calling them together. This is the reason for the requirement that the Congress of the United States must meet at least once a year. The 20th Amendment changed the date of the opening day of the session to January 3, unless Congress sets another date by law.

Section 5

(1) Each House shall be the Judge of the Elections, Returns and Qualifications of its own Members, and a Majority of each shall constitute a Quorum to do Business; but a smaller Number may adjourn from day to day, and may be authorized to compel the Attendance of absent Members, in such Manner, and under such Penalties as each House may provide.

Each house determines if its members are legally qualified to serve and have been elected fairly. In judging the qualifications of its members, each house may consider only the age, citizenship, and residence requirements set forth in the Constitution. In acting on motions to expel a member, however, either house of Congress may consider other matters bearing on that member's fitness for office. A *quorum* is a group large enough to carry on business. Discussion and debate can go on whether a quorum is present or not, as long as a quorum comes in to vote.

(2) Each House may determine the Rules of its Proceedings, punish its Members for disorderly Behaviour, and, with the Concurrence of two thirds, expel a Member.

Each house can expel one of its members by a two-thirds vote. Each house makes its own rules. For example, the House of Representatives puts strict time limits on debate to speed up business. It is much more difficult to end debate in the Senate. A senator may speak as long as he or she wishes unless the Senate votes for *cloture,* a motion to end debate. On most matters, cloture requires a vote of 60 senators, or three-fifths of the total Senate membership.

(3) Each House shall keep a Journal of its Proceedings, and from time to time publish the same, excepting such Parts as may in their Judgment require Secrecy; and the Yeas and Nays of the Members of either House on any question shall, at the Desire of one fifth of those Present, be entered on the Journal.

The House *Journal* and the Senate *Journal* are published at the end of each session of Congress. They list all the bills and resolutions considered during the session, as well as every vote. All messages from the president to Congress also are included. The journals are the only publications required by the Constitution and are considered the official documents for the proceedings of Congress.

(4) Neither House, during the Session of Congress, shall, without the Consent of the other, adjourn for more than three days, nor to any other Place than that in which the two Houses shall be sitting.

Section 6

(1) The Senators and Representatives shall receive a Compensation for their Services, to be ascertained by Law, and paid out of the Treasury of the United States. They shall in all Cases, except Treason, Felony and Breach of the Peace, be privileged from Arrest during their Attendance at the Session of their respective Houses, and in going to and returning from the same; and for any Speech or Debate in either House, they shall not be questioned in any other Place.

The privilege of *immunity* (freedom from arrest) while going to and from congressional business has little importance today. Members of Congress, like anyone else, may be arrested for breaking the law. They may be tried, convicted, and sent to prison.

Congressional immunity from charges of *libel* and *slander* remains important. Libel is an untrue written statement that damages a person's reputation. Slander is a spoken statement that does so. Immunity under the Speech and Debate Clause means that members of Congress may say whatever they wish in connection with congressional business without fear of being sued. This immunity extends to anything said during debate, in an official report, or while voting.

(2) No Senator or Representative shall, during the Time for which he was elected, be appointed to any civil Office under the Authority of the United States which shall have been created, or the Emoluments whereof shall have been encreased during such time; and no Person holding any Office under the United States, shall be a Member of either House during his Continuance in Office.

These provisions keep members of Congress from creating jobs to which they can later be appointed, from raising the salaries of jobs they hope to hold in the future, and from holding office in other branches of government.

In 1909 Senator Philander C. Knox resigned from the Senate to become secretary of state. But the salary of the secretary of state had been increased during Knox's term as senator. In order that Knox might accept the post, Congress withdrew the salary increase for the period of Knox's unfinished term.

Section 7

(1) All Bills for raising Revenue shall originate in the House of Representatives; but the Senate may propose or concur with Amendments as on other Bills.

Tax bills must originate in the House. This tradition came from Britain. There, the lower house—the House of Commons—is more likely to reflect the people's wishes because the people elect its members. They do not elect members of the upper house, the House of Lords. In the United States this rule has little importance since the adoption of the 17th Amendment because the people now elect members of both the Senate and the House. In addition, the Senate can amend a tax bill to such an extent that it

(2) Every Bill which shall have passed the House of Representatives and the Senate, shall, before it becomes a Law, be presented to the President of the United States; If he approve he shall sign it, but if not he shall return it, with his Objections to that House in which it shall have originated, who shall enter the Objections at large on their Journal, and proceed to reconsider it. If after such Reconsideration two thirds of that House shall agree to pass the Bill, it shall be sent, together with the Objections, to the other House, by which it shall likewise be reconsidered, and if approved by two thirds of that House, it shall become a Law. But in all such Cases the Votes of both Houses shall be determined by yeas and Nays, and the Names of the Persons voting for and against the Bill shall be entered on the Journal of each House respectively, If any Bill shall not be returned by the President within ten Days (Sundays excepted) after it shall have been presented to him, the Same shall be a Law, in like Manner as if he had signed it, unless the Congress by their Adjournment prevent its Return, in which Case it shall not be a Law.

A bill passed by Congress goes to the president for the president's signature. If the president disapproves the bill, it must be returned to Congress with a statement of the objections within 10 days, not including Sundays. This action is called a *veto*. Congress can pass a law over the president's veto, or *override* the veto, by a two-thirds vote of each house of those members present. The president can also let a bill become law without signing it merely by letting 10 days pass while Congress is in session. But a bill sent to the president during the last 10 days of a session of Congress cannot become law unless it is signed. If a bill the president dislikes reaches the president near the end of the session, the bill may simply be held unsigned. When Congress adjourns, the bill is killed. This practice is known as a *pocket veto*.

(3) Every Order, Resolution, or Vote to which the Concurrence of the Senate and House of Representatives may be necessary (except on a question of Adjournment) shall be presented to the President of the United States; and before the Same shall take Effect, shall be approved by him, or being disapproved by him, shall be repassed by two thirds of the Senate and House of Representatives, according to the Rules and Limitations prescribed in the Case of a Bill.

Section 8

Powers Granted to Congress

The Congress shall have Power
(1) To lay and collect Taxes, Duties, Imposts and Excises, to pay the Debts and provide for the common Defence and general Welfare of the United States; but all Duties, Imposts and Excises shall be uniform throughout the United States;

Duties are taxes on goods coming into the United States. *Excises* are taxes on sales, use, or production, and sometimes on business procedures or privileges. For example, corporation taxes, cigarette taxes, and amusement taxes are excises. *Imposts* is a general tax term that includes both duties and excises.

(2) To borrow Money on the credit of the United States;

(3) To regulate Commerce with foreign Nations, and among the several States, and with the Indian Tribes;

This section, called the *Commerce Clause*, gives Congress some of its most important powers. The Supreme Court has interpreted *commerce* to mean not only trade but also all kinds of commercial activity. Commerce "among the several States" is usually called *interstate commerce*. The Supreme Court has ruled that interstate commerce includes not only transactions across state boundaries but also any activity that affects commerce in more than one state. The Court has interpreted the word *regulate* to mean *encourage, promote, protect, prohibit,* or *restrain*. As a result, Congress can pass laws and provide funds to improve waterways, to enforce air safety measures, and to forbid interstate shipment of certain goods. It can regulate the movement of people, of trains, of stocks and bonds, and even of television signals. Congress has made it a federal crime to flee across state lines from state or local police. It also has forbidden people who operate interstate facilities or who serve interstate passengers to treat customers unfairly because of race.

(4) To establish an uniform Rule of Naturalization, and uniform Laws on the subject of Bankruptcies throughout the United States;
(5) To coin Money, regulate the Value thereof, and of foreign Coin, and fix the Standard of Weights and Measures;

From this section, along with the section that allows Congress to regulate commerce and to borrow money, Congress gets its right to charter national banks and to establish the Federal Reserve System.

(6) To provide for the Punishment of counterfeiting the Securities and current Coin of the United States;

Securities are government bonds.

(7) To establish Post Offices and post Roads;
(8) To promote the Progress of Science and useful Arts, by securing for limited Times to Authors and Inventors the exclusive Right to their respective Writings and Discoveries;

Photographs and films may also be copyrighted under this rule.

(9) To constitute Tribunals inferior to the supreme Court;

Examples of federal courts "inferior to the supreme Court" include the United States district courts and the United States Courts of Appeals.

(10) To define and punish Piracies and Felonies committed on the high Seas, and Offenses against the Law of Nations;

Congress, rather than the states, has jurisdiction over crimes committed at sea.

(11) To declare War, grant Letters of Marque and Reprisal, and make Rules concerning Captures on Land and Water;

Only Congress can declare war. However, the president, as commander in chief, has engaged the United States in wars without a declaration by Congress. Undeclared wars include the Korean War (1950–1953) and the Vietnam War (1957–1975). *Letters of marque and reprisal* are documents that authorize private vessels to attack enemy shipping.

(12) To raise and support Armies, but no Appropriation of Money to that Use shall be for a longer Term than two Years;
(13) To provide and maintain a Navy;
(14) To make Rules for the Government and Regulation of the land and naval Forces;

(15) To provide for calling forth the Militia to execute the Laws of the Union, suppress Insurrections and repel Invasions;

Congress has given the president power to decide when a state of invasion or *insurrection* (uprising) exists. At such times, the president can call out the National Guard.

(16) To provide for organizing, arming, and disciplining, the Militia, and for governing such Part of them as may be employed in the Service of the United States, reserving to the States respectively, the Appointment of the Officers, and the Authority of training the Militia according to the discipline prescribed by Congress;

The federal government helps the states maintain the militia, also known as the National Guard. Until 1916 the states controlled the militia entirely. That year the National Defense Act provided for federal funding of the guard and for drafting the guard into national service under certain circumstances.

(17) To exercise exclusive Legislation in all Cases whatsoever, over such District (not exceeding ten Miles square) as may, by Cession of particular States, and the Acceptance of Congress, become the Seat of the Government of the United States, and to exercise like Authority over all Places purchased by the Consent of the Legislature of the State in which the Same shall be, for the Erection of Forts, Magazines, Arsenals, dock-Yards and other needful Buildings;— And

This section makes Congress the legislative body not only for the District of Columbia, but also for federal property on which forts, naval bases, arsenals, and other federal works or buildings are located.

(18) To make all Laws which shall be necessary and proper for carrying into Execution the foregoing Powers, and all other Powers vested by this Constitution in the Government of the United States, or in any Department or Officer thereof.

This section, the famous *Necessary and Proper Clause,* allows Congress to deal with many matters not specifically mentioned in the Constitution. As times have changed, Congress

has been able to pass needed laws with few amendments to the Constitution. This flexibility helps explain why the Constitution is one of the oldest written constitutions.

Section 9

Powers Forbidden to Congress

(1) [The Migration or Importation of such Persons as any of the States now existing shall think proper to admit, shall not be prohibited by the Congress prior to the Year one thousand eight hundred and eight, but a Tax or duty may be imposed on such Importation, not exceeding ten dollars for each Person.]

This paragraph refers to the slave trade. Dealers in slaves, as well as some slaveholders, wanted to make sure that Congress could not stop anyone from bringing slaves into the country before the year 1808. That year Congress did ban the importation of slaves.

(2) The Privilege of the Writ of Habeas Corpus shall not be suspended, unless when in Cases of Rebellion or Invasion the public Safety may require it.

A *writ of habeas corpus* is an order that commands people who have a person in custody to bring the person into court to explain why the person is being restrained. If their explanation is unsatisfactory, the judge can order the prisoner released.

(3) No Bill of Attainder or ex post facto Law shall be passed.

A *bill of attainder* is an act passed by a legislature to punish a person without a trial. An *ex post facto law* is one that provides punishment for an act that was not illegal when the act was committed.

(4) No Capitation, [or other direct,] Tax shall be laid, unless in Proportion to the Census or Enumeration herein before directed to be taken.

A *capitation* is a tax collected equally from everyone. It is also called a *head tax* or a *poll tax.* The Supreme Court held that this section prohibits an income tax. The 16th Amendment set aside the Court's decision.

8

(5) No Tax or Duty shall be laid on Articles exported from any State.

In this sentence, *exported* means sent to other states or to foreign countries. The southern states feared that the new government would tax their exports. This sentence forbids such a tax. However, Congress can prohibit shipment of certain items or regulate the conditions of their shipment.

(6) No Preference shall be given by any Regulation of Commerce or Revenue to the Ports of one State over those of another: nor shall Vessels bound to, or from, one State, be obliged to enter, clear, or pay Duties in another.

Congress cannot make laws concerning trade that favor one state over another. Ships going from one state to another need not pay taxes to do so.

(7) No Money shall be drawn from the Treasury, but in Consequence of Appropriations made by Law; and a regular Statement and Account of the Receipts and Expenditures of all public Money shall be published from time to time.

Government money cannot be spent without the consent of Congress. Congress must issue financial statements periodically. Congress authorizes money for most programs in lump sums rather than separately.

(8) No Title of Nobility shall be granted by the United States: And no Person holding any Office of Profit or Trust under them, shall, without the Consent of the Congress, accept of any present, Emolument, Office, or Title, of any kind whatever, from any King, Prince, or foreign State.

Congress cannot give anyone a title of nobility, such as countess or duke. Federal officials may not accept a gift, office, payment, or title from a foreign country without the consent of Congress.

Section 10

Powers Forbidden to the States

(1) No State shall enter into any Treaty, Alliance, or Confederation; grant Letters of Marque and Reprisal; coin Money; emit Bills of Credit; make any Thing but gold and silver Coin a Tender in Payment of Debts; pass any Bill of Attainder, ex post facto Law, or Law impairing the Obligation of Contracts, or grant any Title of Nobility.

(2) No State shall, without the Consent of the Congress, lay any Imposts or Duties on Imports or Exports, except what may be absolutely necessary for executing its inspection Laws: and the net Produce of all Duties and Imposts, laid by any State on Imports or Exports, shall be for the Use of the Treasury of the United States; and all such Laws shall be subject to the Revision and Controul of the Congress.

Without the consent of Congress, a state cannot tax goods entering or leaving the state except for small fees to cover inspection costs. Profits from a tax on interstate commerce go to the federal government.

(3) No State shall, without the Consent of Congress, lay any Duty of Tonnage, keep Troops, or Ships of War in time of Peace, enter into any Agreement or Compact with another State, or with a foreign Power, or engage in War, unless actually invaded, or in such imminent Danger as will not admit of delay.

Only the federal government may make treaties and carry out measures for national defense.

ARTICLE II
The Executive Branch

Section 1

(1) The executive Power shall be vested in a President of the United States of America. He shall hold his Office during the Term of four Years, and, together with the Vice President, chosen for the same Term, be elected, as follows

(2) Each State shall appoint, in such Manner as the Legislature thereof may direct, a Number of Electors, equal to the whole Number of Senators and Representatives to which the State may be entitled in the Congress: but no Senator or Representative, or Person holding an Office of Trust or Profit under the United States, shall be appointed an Elector.

This section establishes the electoral college, a group chosen to elect the president and vice president.

(3) [The Electors shall meet in their respective States, and vote by Ballot for two Persons, of whom one at least shall not be an Inhabitant of the same State with themselves. And they shall make a List of all the Persons voted for, and of the Number of Votes for each; which List they shall sign and certify, and transmit sealed to the Seat of the Government of the United States, directed to the President of the Senate. The President of the Senate shall, in the Presence of the Senate and House of Representatives, open all the Certificates, and the Votes shall then be counted. The Person having the greatest Number of Votes shall be the President, if such Number be a Majority of the whole Number of Electors appointed; and if there be more than one who have such Majority, and have an equal Number of Votes, then the House of Representatives shall immediately chuse by Ballot one of them for President; and if no Person have a Majority, then from the five highest on the List the said House shall in like Manner chuse the President. But in chusing the President, the Votes shall be taken by States, the Representation from each State having one Vote; A quorum for this Purpose shall consist of a Member or Members from two thirds of the States, and a Majority of all the States shall be necessary to a Choice. In every Case, after the Choice of the President, the Person having the greatest Number of Votes of the Electors shall be the Vice President. But if there should remain two or more who have equal Votes, the Senate shall chuse from them by Ballot the Vice President.]

The 12th Amendment changed this procedure for electing the president and vice president.

(4) The Congress may determine the Time of chusing the Electors, and the Day on which they shall give their Votes; which Day shall be the same throughout the United States.

(5) No Person except a natural born Citizen, [or a Citizen of the United States, at the time of the Adoption of this Constitution,] shall be eligible to the Office of President; neither shall any person be eligible to that Office who shall not have attained to the Age of thirty five Years, and been fourteen Years a Resident within the United States.

(6) In Case of the Removal of the President from Office, or of his Death, Resignation, or Inability to discharge the Powers and Duties of the said Office, the Same shall devolve on the Vice President, and the Congress may by Law provide for the Case of Removal, Death, Resignation or Inability, both of the President and Vice President, declaring what Officer shall then act as President, and such Officer shall act accordingly, until the Disability be removed, or a President shall be elected.

On August 9, 1974, President Richard M. Nixon resigned as chief executive and was succeeded by Vice President Gerald Ford. Until then, only death had ever cut short the term of a president. The 25th Amendment provides that the vice president succeeds to the presidency if the president becomes disabled and specifies the conditions of succession.

(7) The President shall, at stated Times, receive for his Services, a Compensation, which shall neither be increased nor diminished during the Period for which he shall have been elected, and he shall not receive within that Period any other Emolument from the United States, or any of them.

The Constitution made it possible for a poor person to become president by providing a salary for that office. The president's salary cannot be raised or lowered during his or her term of office. The chief executive may not receive any other pay from the government.

(8) Before he enter on the Execution of his Office, he shall take the following Oath or Affirmation: —"I do solemnly swear (or affirm) that I will faithfully execute the Office of President of the United States, and will to the best of my Ability, preserve, protect and defend the Constitution of the United States."

The Constitution does not say who shall administer the oath to the newly elected president. President George Washington was sworn in by Robert R. Livingston, then a state official in New York. After that, it became customary for the chief justice of the United States to administer the oath.

Section 2

(1) The President shall be Commander in Chief of the Army and Navy of the United States, and of the Militia of the several States, when called into the actual Service of the United States; he may require the Opinion, in writing, of the principal Officer in each of the executive Departments, upon any Subject relating to the Duties of their respective Offices, and he shall have Power to grant Reprieves and Pardons for Offenses against the United States, except in Cases of Impeachment.

The president's powers as commander in chief are far-reaching. But even in wartime, the president must obey the law of the land.

(2) He shall have Power, by and with the Advice and Consent of the Senate, to make Treaties, provided two thirds of the Senators present concur; and he shall nominate, and by and with the Advice and Consent of the Senate, shall appoint Ambassadors, other public Ministers and Consuls, Judges of the supreme Court, and all other Officers of the United States, whose Appointments are not herein otherwise provided for, and which shall be established by Law: but the Congress may by Law vest the Appointment of such inferior Officers, as they think proper, in the President alone, in the Courts of Law, or in the Heads of Departments.

The framers of the Constitution intended that in some matters the Senate should serve as an advisory body for the president. The president can make treaties and appoint various government officials. But two-thirds of the senators present must approve before a treaty is confirmed. Also, high appointments require approval of more than half the senators present.

(3) The President shall have Power to fill up all Vacancies that may happen during the Recess of the Senate, by granting Commissions which shall expire at the End of their next Session.

This clause means that when the Senate is not in session, the president can make temporary appointments to offices that require senate confirmation.

Section 3

He shall from time to time give to the Congress Information of the State of the Union, and recommend to their Consideration such Measures as he shall judge necessary and expedient; he may, on extraordinary Occasions, convene both Houses, or either of them, and in Case of Dis-

agreement between them, with Respect to the Time of Adjournment, he may adjourn them to such Time as he shall think proper; he shall receive Ambassadors and other public Ministers; he shall take Care that the Laws be faithfully executed, and shall Commission all the Officers of the United States.

The president gives a State of the Union message to Congress each year. Presidents George Washington and John Adams delivered their messages in person. For more than 100 years after that, most presidents sent a written message, which was read in Congress. President Woodrow Wilson delivered his messages in person, as did President Franklin D. Roosevelt and all presidents after Roosevelt. The president's messages often have great influence on public opinion, and thus on Congress.

During the 1800s presidents often called Congress into session. Today Congress is in session most of the time. No president has ever had to adjourn Congress.

The responsibility to "take Care that the Laws be faithfully executed" puts the president at the head of law enforcement for the national government. Every federal official, civilian or military, gets his or her authority from the president.

Section 4

The President, Vice President and all civil Officers of the United States, shall be removed from Office on Impeachment for, and Conviction of, Treason, Bribery, or other high Crimes and Misdemeanors.

ARTICLE III
The Judicial Branch

Section 1

The judicial Power of the United States, shall be vested in one supreme Court, and in such inferior Courts as the Congress may from time to time ordain and establish. The Judges, both of the supreme and inferior Courts, shall hold their Offices during good Behaviour, and shall, at stated Times, receive for their Services, a Compensation, which shall not be diminished during their Continuance in Office.

The Constitution makes every effort to keep the courts independent of both the legislature and the president. The guarantee that judges shall hold office during "good Behaviour" means that, unless they are impeached and convicted, they can hold office for life. This guarantee protects judges from any threat of dismissal by the president during their lifetime. The rule that a judge's salary may not be reduced protects the judge against pressure from Congress, which could otherwise threaten to fix the salary so low that the judge could be forced to resign.

Section 2

(1) The judicial Power shall extend to all Cases, in Law and Equity, arising under this Constitution, the Laws of the United States, and Treaties made, or which shall be made, under their Authority; to all Cases affecting Ambassadors, other public Ministers and Consuls; to all Cases of admiralty and maritime Jurisdiction; to Controversies to which the United States shall be a Party; to Controversies between two or more States; [between a State and Citizens of another State;] between Citizens of different States; between Citizens of the same State claiming Lands under Grants of different States, [and between a State, or the Citizens thereof, and foreign States, Citizens or Subjects.]

The right of the federal courts to handle "Cases . . . arising under this Constitution" is the basis of the Supreme Court's right to declare laws of Congress unconstitutional. This right of "judicial review" was established by Chief Justice John Marshall's historic decision in the case of *Marbury v. Madison* in 1803.

The 11th Amendment set aside the phrase "between a State and Citizens of another State." A citizen of one state cannot sue another state in federal court.

(2) In all Cases affecting Ambassadors, other public Ministers and Consuls, and those in which a State shall be Party, the supreme Court shall have original Jurisdiction. In all the other Cases before mentioned, the supreme Court shall have appellate Jurisdiction, both as to Law and Fact, with such Exceptions, and under such Regulations as the Congress shall make.

The statement that the Supreme Court has *original* jurisdiction in cases affecting the representatives of foreign countries and in cases to which a state is a party means that cases of this kind go directly to the Supreme Court. In other

kinds of cases, the Supreme Court has *appellate jurisdiction*. This means that the cases are tried first in a lower court and may come up to the Supreme Court for review if Congress authorizes an appeal. Congress cannot take away or modify the original jurisdiction of the Supreme Court, but it can take away the right to appeal to that Court or fix the conditions one must meet to present an appeal.

(3) The Trial of all Crimes, except in Cases of Impeachment; shall be by Jury; and such Trial shall be held in the State where the said Crimes shall have been committed; but when not committed within any State, the Trial shall be at such Place or Places as the Congress may by Law have directed.

Section 3

(1) Treason against the United States, shall consist only in levying War against them, or in adhering to their Enemies, giving them Aid and Comfort. No Person shall be convicted of Treason unless on the Testimony of two Witnesses to the same overt Act, or on Confession in open Court.

No person can be convicted of treason against the United States unless he or she confesses in open court, or unless two witnesses testify that he or she has committed a treasonable act. Talking or thinking about committing a treasonable act is not treason.

(2) The Congress shall have Power to declare the Punishment of Treason, but no Attainder of Treason shall work Corruption of Blood, or Forfeiture except during the Life of the Person attainted.

The phrase "no Attainder of Treason shall work Corruption of Blood" means that the family of a traitor does not share the guilt. Formerly, an offender's family could also be punished.

ARTICLE IV
Relation of the States to Each Other

Section 1

Full Faith and Credit shall be given in each State to the public Acts, Records, and judicial Proceedings of every other State; And the Congress may by general Laws prescribe the Manner in which such Acts, Records and Proceedings shall be proved, and the Effect thereof.

This section requires the states to honor one another's laws, records, and court rulings. The rule prevents a person from avoiding justice by leaving a state.

Section 2

(1) The Citizens of each State shall be entitled to all Privileges and Immunities of Citizens in the several States.

This clause means that citizens traveling from state to state are entitled to all the privileges and immunities that automatically go to citizens of those states. Some privileges, such as the right to vote, do not automatically go with citizenship, but require a period of residence and perhaps other qualifications. The word "Citizens" in this provision does not include corporations.

(2) A Person charged in any State with Treason, Felony, or other Crime, who shall flee from Justice, and be found in another State, shall on Demand of the executive Authority of the State from which he fled, be delivered up, to be removed to the State having Jurisdiction of the Crime.

If a person commits a crime in one state and flees to another state, the governor of the state in which the crime was committed can demand that the fugitive be handed over. The process of returning an accused person is called *extradition*. In a few cases, governors have refused to extradite because the crime was committed many years ago or because it was believed that the accused would not get a fair trial in the other state. It is not clear how the federal government could enforce this section.

(3) [No Person held to Service or Labour in one State, under the Laws thereof, escaping into another, shall, in Consequence of any Law or Regulation therein, be discharged from such Service or Labour, but shall be delivered up on Claim of the Party to whom such Service or Labour may be due.]

A "Person held to Service or Labour" was a slave or an *indentured servant* (a person bound by contract to serve someone for several years). No one is now bound to servitude in the United States, so this part of the Constitution no longer

has any force, being superseded by the 13th Amendment.

Section 3

Federal-State Relations

(1) New States may be admitted by the Congress into this Union; but no new State shall be formed or erected within the Jurisdiction of any other State; nor any State be formed by the Junction of two or more States, or Parts of States, without the Consent of the Legislatures of the States concerned as well as of the Congress.

New states cannot be formed by dividing or joining existing states without the consent of the state legislatures and Congress. During the Civil War (1861–1865), Virginia fought for the Confederacy, but people in the western part of the state supported the Union. After West Virginia split from Virginia, Congress accepted the state on the ground that Virginia had rebelled.

(2) The Congress shall have Power to dispose of and make all needful Rules and Regulations respecting the Territory or other Property belonging to the United States; and nothing in this Constitution shall be so construed as to Prejudice any Claims of the United States, or of any particular State.

Section 4

The United States shall guarantee to every State in this Union a Republican Form of Government, and shall protect each of them against Invasion; and on Application of the Legislature, or of the Executive (when the Legislature cannot be convened) against domestic Violence.

This section requires the federal government to make sure that every state has a "Republican Form of Government." A *republican government* is one in which the people elect representatives to govern. The Supreme Court ruled that Congress, not the courts, must decide whether a government is republican. According to the Court, if Congress admits a state's senators and representatives, that action indicates that Congress considers the government republican. The legislature or governor of a state can request federal aid to deal with riots or other internal violence.

ARTICLE V

Amending the Constitution

The Congress, whenever two thirds of both Houses shall deem it necessary, shall propose Amendments to this Constitution, or, on the Application of the Legislatures of two thirds of the several States, shall call a Convention for proposing Amendments, which, in either Case, shall be valid to all Intents and Purposes, as Part of this Constitution, when ratified by the Legislatures of three fourths of the several States, or by Conventions in three fourths thereof, as the one or the other Mode of Ratification may be proposed by the Congress; Provided [that no Amendment which may be made prior to the Year One thousand eight hundred and eight shall in any Manner affect the first and fourth Clauses in the Ninth Section of the first Article; and] that no State, without its Consent, shall be deprived of its equal Suffrage in the Senate.

Amendments may be proposed by a two-thirds vote of each house of Congress or by a national convention called by Congress at the request of two-thirds of the states. To become part of the Constitution, amendments must be *ratified* (approved) by the legislatures of three-fourths of the states or by conventions in three-fourths of the states.

The framers of the Constitution purposely made it hard to put through an amendment. Congress has considered more than 7,000 amendments, but it has passed only 33 and submitted them to the states. Of these, only 26 have been ratified. Only one amendment, the 21st, was ratified by state conventions. All the others were ratified by state legislatures.

The Constitution sets no time limit during which the states must ratify a proposed amendment. But the courts have held that amendments must be ratified within a "reasonable time" and that Congress decides what is reasonable. Since the early 1900s most proposed amendments have included a requirement that ratification be obtained within seven years.

ARTICLE VI

National Debts

(1) All Debts contracted and Engagements entered into, before the Adoption of this Constitution, shall be as valid against the United States under this Constitution, as under the Confederation.

This section promises that all debts and obligations made by the United States before the adoption of the Constitution will be honored.

Supremacy of the National Government

(2) This Constitution, and the Laws of the United States which shall be made in Pursuance thereof; and all Treaties made, or which shall be made, under the Authority of the United States, shall be the supreme Law of the Land; and the Judges in every State shall be bound thereby, any Thing in the Constitution or Laws of any State to the Contrary notwithstanding.

This section, known as the *Supremacy Clause,* has been called *the linchpin of the Constitution*—that is, the part that keeps the entire structure from falling apart. It means simply that when state laws conflict with national laws, the national laws are superior. It also means that, to be valid, a national law must be in conformity with the Constitution.

(3) The Senators and Representatives before mentioned, and the Members of the several State Legislatures, and all executive and judicial Officers, both of the United States and of the several States, shall be bound by Oath or Affirmation, to support this Constitution; but no religious Test shall ever be required as a Qualification to any Office or public Trust under the United States.

This section requires both federal and state officials to give supreme allegiance to the Constitution of the United States rather than to the constitution of any state. The section also forbids any kind of religious test for holding office. This provision applies only to the national government, but the 14th Amendment applies the same rule to state and local governments.

ARTICLE VII

Ratifying the Constitution

The Ratification of the Conventions of nine States, shall be sufficient for the Establishment of this Constitution between the States so ratifying the Same.

Done in Convention by the Unanimous Consent of the States present the Seventeenth Day of September in the Year of our Lord one thousand seven hundred and Eighty seven and of the Independence of the United States of America the Twelfth. In Witness whereof We have hereunto subscribed our Names,

Go. Washington - President
and deputy from Virginia
Attest William Jackson Secretary

Delaware	Geo: Read Gunning Bedford jun John Dickinson Richard Bassett Jaco: Broom
Maryland	James McHenry Dan of St Thos. Jenifer Danl Carroll
Virginia	John Blair— James Madison JR.
North Carolina	Wm. Blount Richd. Dobbs Spaight Hu Williamson
South Carolina	J. Rutledge Charles Cotesworth Pinckney Charles Pinckney Pierce Butler
Georgia	William Few Abr Baldwin
New Hampshire	John Langdon Nicholas Gilman
Massachusetts	Nathaniel Gorham Rufus King
Connecticut	Wm. Saml. Johnson Roger Sherman
New York	Alexander Hamilton
New Jersey	Wil· Livingston David Brearley Wm. Paterson Jona: Dayton
Pennsylvania	B Franklin Thomas Mifflin Robt Morris Geo. Clymer Thos. FitzSimons Jared Ingersoll James Wilson Gouv Morris

AMENDMENTS TO THE CONSTITUTION

ARTICLES in addition to, and amendment of, the Constitution of the United States of America, proposed by Congress, and ratified by the Legislatures of the several states, pursuant to the fifth article of the original Constitution.

The first 10 amendments, known as the Bill of Rights, were proposed on September 25, 1789, and ratified on December 15, 1791. Originally, the amendments applied only to the federal government. But the 14th Amendment declares that no state can deprive any person of life, liberty, or property without "due process of law." The Supreme Court has interpreted those words to mean that most of the Bill of Rights applies to the states as well.

AMENDMENT 1

Freedom of Religion, Speech, and the Press; Rights of Assembly and Petition

Congress shall make no law respecting an establishment of religion, or prohibiting the free exercise thereof; or abridging the freedom of speech, or of the press, or the right of the people peaceably to assemble, and to petition the Government for a redress of grievances.

Many countries have made one religion the *established* (official) church and supported it with government funds. This amendment forbids Congress to set up or in any way provide for an established church. It has been interpreted to forbid government endorsement of or aid to religious doctrines. In addition, Congress may not pass laws limiting worship, speech, or the press, or preventing people from meeting peacefully. Congress also may not keep people from asking for relief from unfair treatment. The Supreme Court has interpreted the 14th Amendment as applying the First Amendment to the states.

The rights protected by this amendment have limits. For example, the guarantee of freedom of religion does not mean that all religious practices must be allowed. In the 1800s some Mormons believed that it was a man's religious duty to have more than one wife. The Supreme Court ruled that Mormons had to obey the laws forbidding that practice.

AMENDMENT 2

Right to Bear Arms

A well regulated Militia, being necessary to the security of a free State, the right of the people to keep and bear Arms, shall not be infringed.

This amendment prohibits only the national government from limiting the right to carry weapons. The amendment was adopted so that Congress could not disarm a state militia.

AMENDMENT 3

Housing of Soldiers

No Soldier shall, in time of peace be quartered in any house, without the consent of the Owner, nor in time of war, but in a manner to be prescribed by law.

This amendment grew directly out of an old complaint against the British, who had forced people to take soldiers into their homes.

AMENDMENT 4

Search and Arrest Warrants

The right of the people to be secure in their persons, houses, papers, and effects, against unreasonable searches and seizures, shall not be violated, and no Warrants shall issue, but upon probable cause, supported by Oath or affirmation, and particularly describing the place to be searched, and the persons or things to be seized.

This measure does not forbid authorities to search, to seize goods, or to arrest people. It simply requires that in most cases the authorities first obtain a search warrant from a judge. The Supreme Court has held that evidence obtained in violation of the Fourth Amendment may not be admitted in a criminal trial.

AMENDMENT 5

Rights in Criminal Cases

No person shall be held to answer for a capital, or otherwise infamous crime, unless on a presentment or indictment of a Grand Jury, except in cases arising in the land or naval forces, or in the Militia, when in actual service in time of War or public danger; nor shall any person be subject for the same offence to be twice put in jeopardy of life or limb, nor shall be compelled in any criminal case to be a witness against himself, nor be deprived of life, liberty, or property, without due process of law; nor shall private property be taken for public use without just compensation.

A *capital crime* is one punishable by death. An *infamous crime* is one punishable by death or imprisonment. This amendment guarantees that no one has to stand trial for such a federal crime unless he or she has been *indicted* (accused) by a *grand jury*. A grand jury is a special group selected to decide whether there is enough evidence against a person to hold a trial. A person cannot be *put in double jeopardy* (tried twice) for the same offense by the same government. But a person may be tried a second time if a jury cannot agree on a verdict, if a mistrial is declared for some other reason, or if the person requests a new trial. The amendment also guarantees that people cannot be forced to testify against themselves.

The statement that no person shall be deprived of life, liberty, or property "without due process of law" expresses one of the most important rules of the Constitution. The same words are in the 14th Amendment as restrictions on the power of the states. The phrase expresses the idea that a person's life, liberty, and property are not subject to the uncontrolled power of the government. This idea can be traced to the Magna Carta, which provided that the king could not imprison or harm a person "except by the lawful judgment of his peers or by the law of the land." Due process is a vague rule, and the Supreme Court has applied it to widely different cases. Until the mid-1900s, the Court used the due process rule to strike down laws that prevented people from using their property as they wished. For example, the Court overturned the Missouri Compromise, which prohibited slavery in the United States territories. The Court said the compromise unjustly prevented slave owners from taking slaves—their property—into the territories. Today the courts use the due process rule to strike down laws that interfere with personal liberty.

The amendment also forbids the government to take a person's property without fair payment. The government's right to take property for public use is called *eminent domain*. Governments use it to acquire land for highways, schools, and other public facilities.

AMENDMENT 6

Rights to a Fair Trial

In all criminal prosecutions, the accused shall enjoy the right to a speedy and public trial, by an impartial jury of the State and district wherein the crime shall have been committed; which district shall have been previously ascertained by law, and to be informed of the nature and cause of the accusation; to be confronted with the witnesses against him; to have compulsory process for obtaining witnesses in his favor, and to have the assistance of counsel for his defence.

A person accused of crime must have a prompt, public trial by an open-minded jury. The requirement for a speedy and public trial grew out of the fact that some political trials in Britain had been delayed for years and then were held in secret. Accused individuals must be informed of the charges against them and must be allowed to meet the witnesses against them face to face. Otherwise, innocent persons may be punished if a court allows the testimony of unknown witnesses to be used as evidence. This amendment guarantees that individuals on trial can face and cross-examine those who have accused them. They may be able to show that their accusers lied or made a mistake. Finally, accused persons must have a lawyer to defend them if they want one. If a criminal defendant is unable to afford a lawyer, the Supreme Court has held that one must be appointed to represent the accused individual.

AMENDMENT 7

Rights in Civil Cases

In Suits at common law, where the value in controversy shall exceed twenty dollars, the right of trial by jury shall be preserved, and no fact tried by a jury shall be otherwise re-examined in any Court of the United States, than according to the rules of the common law.

The framers of the Constitution considered the right to jury trial extremely important. In the Sixth Amendment they provided for jury trials in criminal cases. In the Seventh Amendment they provided for such trials in civil suits where the amount contested exceeds $20. The amendment applies only to federal courts. But most state constitutions also call for jury trials in civil cases.

AMENDMENT 8

Bails, Fines, and Punishments

Excessive bail shall not be required, nor excessive fines imposed, nor cruel and unusual punishments inflicted.

Bails, fines, and punishments must be fair and humane. In the case of *Furman v. Georgia,* the Supreme Court ruled in 1972 that capital punishment, as it was then imposed, violated this amendment. The Court held that the death penalty was cruel and unusual punishment because it was not applied fairly and uniformly. After that decision, many states adopted new capital-punishment laws designed to meet the Supreme Court's objections. The Court has ruled that the death penalty may be imposed if certain standards are applied to guard against arbitrary results in capital cases.

AMENDMENT 9

Rights Retained by the People

The enumeration in the Constitution of certain rights shall not be construed to deny or disparage others retained by the people.

Some people feared that the listing of some rights in the Bill of Rights would be interpreted to mean that other rights not listed were not protected. The amendment was adopted to prevent such an interpretation.

AMENDMENT 10

Powers Retained by the States and the People

The powers not delegated to the United States by the Constitution, nor prohibited by it to the States, are reserved to the States respectively, or to the people.

This amendment was adopted to reassure people that the national government would not swallow up the states. It confirms that the states or the people retain all powers not given to the national government. For example, the states have authority over such matters as marriage and divorce. But the Constitution says that the federal government can make any laws "necessary and proper" to carry out its specific powers. This rule makes it hard to determine the exact rights of the states.

AMENDMENT 11

Lawsuits Against States

The Judicial power of the United States shall not be construed to extend to any suit in law or equity, commenced or prosecuted against one of the United States by Citizens of another State, or by Citizens or Subjects of any Foreign State.

This amendment was proposed on March 4, 1794, and ratified on February 7, 1795. The amendment makes it impossible for a citizen of one state to sue another state in federal court. The 11th Amendment resulted from the 1793 case of *Chisholm v. Georgia,* in which a man from South Carolina sued the state of Georgia over an inheritance. Georgia argued that it could not be sued in federal court, but the Supreme Court ruled that the state could be. Georgia then led a movement to add this amendment to the Constitution. However, individuals can still sue state authorities in federal court for depriving them of their constitutional rights.

AMENDMENT 12

Election of the President and Vice President

The Electors shall meet in their respective states, and vote by ballot for President and Vice-President, one of whom, at least, shall not be an inhabitant of the same state with themselves; they shall name in their ballots the person voted for as President, and in distinct ballots the person voted for as Vice-President, and they shall make distinct lists of all persons voted for as President, and of all persons voted for as Vice-President, and of the number of votes for each, which lists they shall sign and certify, and transmit sealed to the seat of the government of the United States, directed to the President of the Senate;—The President of the Senate shall, in the presence of the Senate and House of Representatives, open all the certificates and the votes shall then be counted;—The Person having the greatest number of votes for President, shall be the President, if such number be a majority of the whole number of Electors appointed; and if no person have such majority, then from the persons having the highest numbers not exceeding three on the list of those voted for as President, the House of Representatives shall choose immediately, by ballot, the President. But in choosing the President, the votes shall be taken by states, the representation from each state having one vote; a quorum for this purpose shall consist of a member or members from two-thirds of the states, and a majority of all the states shall be necessary to a choice. [And if the House of Representatives shall not choose a President whenever the right of choice shall devolve upon them, before the fourth day of March next following, then the Vice-President shall act as President, as in the case of the death or other constitutional disability of the President.]—The person having the greatest number of votes as Vice-President, shall be the Vice-President, if such number be a majority of the whole number of Electors appointed, and if no person have a majority, then from the two highest numbers on the list, the Senate shall choose the Vice-President; a quorum for the purpose shall consist of two-thirds of the whole number of Senators, and a majority of the whole number shall be necessary to a choice. But no person constitutionally ineligible to the office of President shall be eligible to that of Vice-President of the United States.

The 12th amendment was proposed on December 9, 1803, and ratified on July 27, 1804. It provides that members of the electoral college, called *electors,* vote for one person as president and another as vice president. The amendment resulted from the election of 1800. At that time each elector voted for two persons, not saying which was to be president and which vice president. The person who received the most votes became president; the runner-up became vice president. Thomas Jefferson, the presidential candidate, and Aaron Burr, the vice presidential candidate, received the same number of votes. The tie threw the election into the House of Representatives. The House chose Jefferson. The House has chosen one other president—John Quincy Adams—in 1825.

AMENDMENT 13
Abolition of Slavery

Section 1

Neither slavery nor involuntary servitude, except as a punishment for crime whereof the party shall have been duly convicted, shall exist within the United States, or any place subject to their jurisdiction.

This amendment was proposed on January 31, 1865, and ratified on December 6, 1865. President Abraham Lincoln's Emancipation Proclamation of 1863 had declared slaves free in the Confederate States still in rebellion. This amendment completed the abolition of slavery in the United States.

Section 2

Congress shall have power to enforce this article by appropriate legislation.

AMENDMENT 14
Civil Rights

Section 1

All persons born or naturalized in the United States and subject to the jurisdiction thereof, are citizens of the United States and of the State wherein they reside. No State shall make or enforce any law which shall abridge the privileges or immunities of citizens of the United States; nor shall any State deprive any person of life, liberty, or property, without due process of law; nor deny to any person within its jurisdiction the equal protection of the laws.

This amendment was proposed on June 13, 1866, and ratified on July 9, 1868. The principal purpose of the amendment was to make former slaves citizens of both the United States and the state in which they lived. The amendment also forbids the states to deny equal rights to any person. The terms of the amendment clarify how citizenship is acquired. State citizenship is a by-product of national citizenship. By living in a state, every United States citizen automatically becomes a citizen of that state as well. All persons *naturalized* (granted citizenship) according to law are United States citizens. Anyone born in the United States is also a citizen regardless of the nationality of his or her parents, unless they are diplomatic representatives of another country or enemies during a wartime occupation. The amendment does not grant citizenship to Indians on reservations, but Congress passed a law that did so.

The phrase "due process of law" has been construed to forbid the states to violate most rights protected by the Bill of Rights. It has also been interpreted as protecting other rights by its own force. The statement that a state cannot deny anyone "equal protection of the laws" has provided the basis for many Supreme Court rulings on civil rights. For example, the Court has outlawed segregation in public schools. The justices declared that "equal protection" means a state must make sure all children, regardless of race, have an equal opportunity for education.

Section 2

Representatives shall be apportioned among the several States according to their respective numbers, counting the whole number of persons in each State, [excluding Indians not taxed.] But when the right to vote at any election for the choice of electors for President and Vice President of the United States, Representatives in Congress, the Executive and Judicial officers of a State, or the members of the Legislature thereof, is denied to any of the [male] inhabitants of such State, being [twenty-one] years of age, and citizens of the United States, or in any way abridged, except for participation in rebellion, or other crime, the basis of representation therein shall be reduced in the proportion which the number of such [male] citizens shall bear to the whole number of [male citizens twenty-one] years of age in such State.

This section proposes a penalty for states that refuse to give the vote in federal elections to all who qualify. States that restrict voting can have their representation in Congress cut down. This penalty has never been used. The section has been set aside by the 19th and 26th amendments.

Section 3

No person shall be a Senator or Representative in Congress, or elector of President and Vice

President, or hold any office, civil or military, under the United States, or under any State, who, having previously taken an oath, as a member of Congress, or as an officer of the United States, or as a member of any State legislature, or as an executive or judicial officer of any State, to support the Constitution of the United States, shall have engaged in insurrection or rebellion against the same, or given aid or comfort to the enemies thereof. But Congress may by a vote of two-thirds of each House, remove such disability.

This section is of historical interest only. Its purpose was to keep federal officers who joined the Confederacy from becoming federal officers again. Congress could vote to overlook such a record.

Section 4

The validity of the public debt of the United States, authorized by law, including debts incurred for payment of pensions and bounties for services in suppressing insurrection or rebellion, shall not be questioned. But neither the United States nor any State shall assume or pay any debt or obligation incurred in aid of insurrection or rebellion against the United States, or any claim for the loss or emancipation of any slave; but all such debts, obligations and claims shall be held illegal and void.

This section ensured that the Union's Civil War debt would be paid but voided debts run up by the Confederacy during the war. The section also said that slave owners would not be paid for slaves who were freed.

Section 5

The Congress shall have power to enforce, by appropriate legislation, the provisions of this article.

AMENDMENT 15
African American Suffrage

Section 1

The right of citizens of the United States to vote shall not be denied or abridged by the United States or by any State on account of race, color, or previous condition of servitude.

This amendment was proposed on February 26, 1869, and ratified on February 3, 1870. African Americans who had been slaves became citizens under the terms of the 14th Amendment. The 15th Amendment does not specifically say that they must be allowed to vote. The states are free to set qualifications for voters. But the amendment says that a voter cannot be denied the ballot because of race. Some states, however, have attempted to do this indirectly. Such measures have been struck down by Supreme Court decisions, federal and state laws, and the 24th Amendment.

Section 2

The Congress shall have power to enforce this article by appropriate legislation.

AMENDMENT 16

Income Taxes

The Congress shall have power to lay and collect taxes on incomes, from whatever source derived, without apportionment among the several States, and without regard to any census or enumeration.

This amendment was proposed on July 12, 1909, and ratified on February 3, 1913. In 1894 Congress passed an income tax law, but the Supreme Court declared the law unconstitutional. This amendment authorized Congress to levy such a tax.

AMENDMENT 17

Direct Election of Senators

(1) The Senate of the United States shall be composed of two Senators from each State, elected by the people thereof, for six years; and each Senator shall have one vote. The electors in each State shall have the qualifications requisite for electors of the most numerous branch of the State legislatures.
(2) When vacancies happen in the representation of any State in the Senate, the executive authority of such State shall issue writs of election to

fill such vacancies: Provided, That the legislature of any State may empower the executive thereof to make temporary appointments until the people fill the vacancies by election as the legislature may direct.

[(3) This amendment shall not be so construed as to affect the election or term of any Senator chosen before it becomes valid as part of the Constitution.]

This amendment was proposed on May 13, 1912, and ratified on April 8, 1913. It takes the power of electing the senators of a state from the state legislature and gives it to the people of the state.

AMENDMENT 18
Prohibition of Liquor

Section 1

[After one year from the ratification of this article the manufacture, sale, or transportation of intoxicating liquors within, the importation thereof into, or the exportation thereof from the United States and all territory subject to the jurisdiction thereof for beverage purposes is hereby prohibited.

Section 2

The Congress and the several States shall have concurrent power to enforce this article by appropriate legislation.

Section 3

This article shall be inoperative unless it shall have been ratified as an amendment to the Constitution by the legislatures of the several States, as provided in the Constitution, within seven years from the date of the submission hereof to the States by the Congress.]

This amendment, the Prohibition Amendment, was proposed on December 18, 1917, and ratified on January 16, 1919. It forbade people to make, sell, or transport liquor. It was repealed by the 21st Amendment in 1933.

AMENDMENT 19
Women's Suffrage
Section 1

The right of citizens of the United States to vote shall not be denied or abridged by the United States or by any State on account of sex.

Section 2

Congress shall have power to enforce this article by appropriate legislation.

This amendment was proposed on June 4, 1919, and ratified on August 18, 1920. Amendments giving women the right to vote were introduced in Congress for more than 40 years before this one was passed.

AMENDMENT 20
Terms of the President and Congress
Section 1

The terms of the President and Vice President shall end at noon, on the 20th day of January, and the terms of Senators and Representatives at noon on the 3d day of January, of the years in which such terms would have ended if this article had not been ratified; and the terms of their successors shall then begin.

Section 2

The Congress shall assemble at least once in every year, and such meeting shall begin at noon on the 3d day of January, unless they shall by law appoint a different day.

Section 3

If, at the time fixed for the beginning of the term of the President, the President elect shall have died, the Vice President elect shall become President. If a President shall not have been chosen before the time fixed for the beginning of his term, or if the President elect shall have failed to qualify, then the Vice President elect shall act as President until a President shall have qualified; and the Congress may by law provide for the case wherein neither a President elect nor a Vice President elect shall have qualified, declaring who shall then act as President, or the manner in which one who is to act shall be selected, and such person shall act accordingly until a President or Vice President shall have qualified.

Section 4

The Congress may by law provide for the case of the death of any of the persons from whom the House of Representatives may choose a President whenever the right of choice shall have devolved upon them, and for the case of the death of any of the persons from whom the Senate may choose a Vice President whenever the right of choice shall have devolved upon them.

Section 5

[Sections 1 and 2 shall take effect on the 15th day of October following the ratification of this article.

Section 6

This article shall be inoperative unless it shall have been ratified as an amendment to the Constitution by the legislatures of three-fourths of the several States within seven years from the date of its submission.]

This amendment was proposed on March 2, 1932, and ratified on January 23, 1933. The amendment, called the *Lame Duck Amendment,* moves the date that newly elected presidents and members of Congress take office closer to election time. A *lame duck* is a government official who continues to serve in office though not reelected to another term. Before the amendment came into force, defeated senators and representatives continued to hold office for four months before their successors took over.

AMENDMENT 21
Repeal of Prohibition

Section 1

The eighteenth article of amendment to the Constitution of the United States is hereby repealed.

Section 2

The transportation or importation into any State, Territory, or possession of the United States for delivery or use therein of intoxicating liquors, in violation of the laws thereof, is hereby prohibited.

Section 3

This article shall be inoperative unless it shall have been ratified as an amendment to the Constitution by conventions in the several States, as provided in the Constitution, within seven years from the date of the submission hereof to the States by the Congress.

The 21st amendment was proposed on February 20, 1933, and ratified on December 5, 1933. The amendment repeals the 18th Amendment. Section 2 promises federal help to "dry" states in enforcing their own prohibition laws.

AMENDMENT 22
Limitation of Presidents to Two Terms

Section 1

No person shall be elected to the office of the President more than twice, and no person who has held the office of President, or acted as President, for more than two years of a term to which some other person was elected President shall be elected to the office of the President more than once. [But this Article shall not apply to any person holding the office of President when this Article was proposed by the Congress, and shall not prevent any person who may be holding the office of President, or acting as President, during the term within which this Article becomes operative from holding the office of President or acting as President during the remainder of such term.

Section 2

This Article shall be inoperative unless it shall have been ratified as an amendment to the Constitution by the legislatures of three-fourths of the several States within seven years from the date of its submission to the States by the Congress.]

This amendment was proposed on March 24, 1947, and ratified on February 27, 1951. It provides that no person can be elected president more than twice. No one who has served as president for more than two years of someone else's term can be elected more than once. The amendment was supported by people who thought President Franklin D. Roosevelt should not serve four terms. No other president had run for election to more than two consecutive terms.

AMENDMENT 23
Suffrage in the District of Columbia

Section 1

The District constituting the seat of Government of the United States shall appoint in such manner as the Congress may direct:

A number of electors of President and Vice President equal to the whole number of Senators and Representatives in Congress to which the District would be entitled if it were a State, but in no event more than the least populous State; they shall be in addition to those appointed by the States, but they shall be considered, for the purposes of the election of President and Vice President, to be electors appointed by a State; and they shall meet in the District and perform such duties as provided by the twelfth article of amendment.

Section 2

The Congress shall have power to enforce this article by appropriate legislation.

This amendment was proposed on June 16, 1960, and ratified on March 29, 1961. It allows citizens of the District of Columbia to vote in presidential elections. However, they cannot vote for members of Congress.

AMENDMENT 24
Poll Taxes

Section 1

The right of citizens of the United States to vote in any primary or other election for President or Vice President, for electors for President or Vice President, or for Senator or Representative in Congress, shall not be denied or abridged by the United States or any State by reason of failure to pay any poll tax or other tax.

Section 2

The Congress shall have power to enforce this article by appropriate legislation.

This amendment was proposed on August 27, 1962, and ratified on January 23, 1964. It forbids making voters pay a *poll tax* before they can vote in a national election. A poll tax, or *head tax,* is a tax collected equally from everyone. Some states once used such taxes to keep poor people and African Americans from voting. The term *poll tax* does not mean a tax on voting. It comes from the old English word *poll,* meaning *head*. The Supreme Court has interpreted the 14th Amendment as forbidding the imposition of a poll tax in state elections.

AMENDMENT 25
Presidential Disability and Succession

Section 1

In case of the removal of the President from office or of his death or resignation, the Vice President shall become President.

This amendment was proposed on July 6, 1965, and ratified on February 10, 1967.

Section 2

Whenever there is a vacancy in the office of the Vice President, the President shall nominate a Vice President who shall take office upon confirmation by a majority vote of both Houses of Congress.

This section provides for filling a vacancy in the vice presidency. In 1973 Gerald R. Ford became the first person chosen vice president under the terms of the amendment. He was nominated by President Richard M. Nixon after Vice President Spiro T. Agnew resigned. In 1974 Nixon resigned and Ford became president.

Nelson A. Rockefeller then became vice president under the new procedure. For the first time the United States had both a president and vice president who had not been elected to their offices. Before this amendment, vacancies in the vice presidency remained unfilled until the next presidential election.

Section 3

Whenever the President transmits to the President pro tempore of the Senate and the Speaker of the House of Representatives his written declaration that he is unable to discharge the powers and duties of his office, and until he transmits to them a written declaration to the contrary, such powers and duties shall be discharged by the Vice President as Acting President.

This section provides that the vice president succeeds to the presidency if the president becomes disabled.

Section 4

Whenever the Vice President and a majority of either the principal officers of the executive departments or of such other body as Congress may by law provide, transmit to the President pro tempore of the Senate and the Speaker of the House of Representatives their written declaration that the President is unable to discharge the powers and duties of his office, the Vice President shall immediately assume the powers and duties of the office as Acting President.

Thereafter, when the President transmits to the President pro tempore of the Senate and the Speaker of the House of Representatives his written declaration that no inability exists, he shall resume the powers and duties of his office unless the Vice President and a majority of either the principal officers of the executive department or of such other body as Congress may by law provide, transmit within four days to the President pro tempore of the Senate and the Speaker of the House of Representatives their written declaration that the President is unable

to discharge the powers and duties of his office. Thereupon Congress shall decide the issue, assembling within forty-eight hours for that purpose if not in session. If the Congress, within twenty-one days after receipt of the latter written declaration, or, if Congress is not in session, within twenty-one says after Congress is required to assemble, determines by two-thirds vote of both Houses that the President is unable to discharge the powers and duties of his office, the Vice President shall continue to discharge the same as Acting President; otherwise, the President shall resume the powers and duties of his office.

AMENDMENT 26
Suffrage for 18-Year-Olds
Section 1

The right of citizens of the United States, who are eighteen years of age or older, to vote shall not be denied or abridged by the United States or by any State on account of age.

Section 2

The Congress shall have power to enforce this article by appropriate legislation.

This amendment was proposed on March 23, 1971, and ratified on July 1, 1971. The amendment grants the vote to citizens 18 years of age or older.

AMENDMENT 27
Congressional Pay Raises

No law, varying the compensation for the services of the Senators and Representatives, shall take effect until an election of Representatives shall have intervened.

Any increase in congressional pay does not go into effect until after the next regular election of the House of Representatives.

CONSTITUTION
ACTIVITY
WORKSHEETS

DEVELOPING YOUR VOCABULARY

Directions: The following words are found in the Constitution. Write a definition for each word in the space provided. If you need help, there is a glossary at the back of this activity book. Then use some of the words to write a paragraph describing how the Constitution affects your life.

1. Domestic Tranquility _____

_____

2. Posterity _____

_____

3. Ordain _____

_____

4. Apportion _____

_____

5. Welfare _____

_____

6. Concurrence _____

_____

7. Habeas corpus _____

_____

8. Jurisdiction _____

_____

9. Infringe _____

_____

10. Deprive _____

_____

11. Impartial _____

_____

12. Redress _____

_____

Your Paragraph _____

_____

_____

_____

_____

OUTLINING THE CONSTITUTION

Directions: Review Articles I-III of the Constitution and complete the following outline.

I. Purpose of establishing the Constitution

    A. _____

    B. _____

    C. _____

    D. _____

    E. _____

    F. _____

II. Legislative branch

    A. Qualifications for House of Representatives

        1. _____

        2. _____

        3. _____

    B. Qualifications for Senate

        1. _____

        2. _____

        3. _____

    C. Five powers delegated to Congress

        1. _____

        2. _____

        3. _____

        4. _____

        5. _____

        _____

        _____

        _____

        _____

OUTLINING THE CONSTITUTION (continued)

D. Four powers denied to Congress

  1. _____

  2. _____

  3. _____

  4. _____

     _____

     _____

     _____

III. Executive branch
  A. Presidential qualifications

  1. _____

  2. _____

  3. _____
  B. Three powers of the president

  1. _____

  2. _____

  3. _____

IV. Judicial branch
  A. Five kinds of cases heard by federal courts

  1. _____

  2. _____

  3. _____

  4. _____

  5. _____

THE CONGRESS AT WORK

Directions: Read Article I, Sections 4–8 of the Constitution. Then complete the sentences below.

1. The life of a Congress is considered to last _____ years. Its regular session begins on _____ of each year. It remains in session until its members _____. The president can call a _____ session of Congress if it is deemed necessary.

2. A majority of the members of each house must be present to conduct business. This majority is called a _____. At the present time this majority consists of _____ members in the House and _____ members in the Senate.

3. Neither house can adjourn for more than _____ days without the consent of the other. Both houses must meet in the same _____.

4. Members of both houses are free from _____ during their attendance at the session of their respective houses.

5. All bills for raising revenue must begin in the _____, but the _____ has the right to propose _____.

6. All bills that have passed the House and the Senate must be sent to the _____. If he or she approves the bill, he or she will _____ it. If not, it may be returned with the objections to the house where the bill originated. If both houses vote by a two-thirds margin to approve the bill anyway, it then becomes a _____.

7. If the president lets a bill sit for _____ days while Congress is in session, it will become a law even if the president does not sign it. If Congress adjourns during this period, the president can kill the bill by doing nothing. This is known as a _____.

8. The powers of Congress include the right to constitute tribunals _____ to the _____, to call forth the _____, and to make all laws which shall be _____ and _____ for carrying into execution the other powers of Congress.

CONSTITUTIONAL WORD PUZZLE

Directions: Use the clues listed below to complete the word puzzle.

1.   **T** __ __ __ __ __
2.   __ **H** __ __ __
3.   __ __ **E** __ __ __
4.   __ __ __ **C** __ __ __
5.   __ __ __ **O** __ __ __ __ __ __
6.   __ __ __ **N** __ __
7.   **S** __ __ __ __ __
8.   __ __ __ __ __ **T** __ __
9.   __ __ __ __ __ __ __ __ **I** __ __ __ __
10.   __ __ __ **T** __ __ __
11.   __ __ __ **U** __ __ __ __ __
12.   __ __ __ __ **T** __ __
13.   __ __ __ __ __ __ **I** __ __
14.   __ __ **O** __ __ __ __
15.   __ __ __ **N** __ __

Clues

1. Waging war against the United States or giving aid and comfort to enemies of the United States
2. Minimum age of a United States senator
3. Opening statement of goals and objectives
4. Power vested in the courts
5. Kind of law that is expressly forbidden by the Constitution
6. All bills for raising _____ must originate in the House of Representatives.
7. Kind of trade that could not be prohibited by Congress before 1808
8. Powers vested in the Congress of the United States
9. President of the Senate
10. Congress and states are denied the power to grant _____ of nobility.
11. The number of representatives that each state is entitled to is based on this.
12. People who were once elected by state legislatures
13. A power vested in the president of the United States
14. Has the power to lay and collect taxes, duties, imposts, and excises
15. The president is the _____ in chief of the army and navy.

CHECKS AND BALANCES

Directions: Listed below are specific checks by which one branch of government can exert some control over another branch. Write who is applying the check on whom in the space provided. Use "E" for executive, "J" for judicial, and "L" for legislative. For example, E over J (executive over judicial) or J over L (judicial over legislative).

1. Remove judges from office _____

2. Veto bills _____

3. Appoint judges _____

4. Override veto _____

5. Call special sessions _____

6. Control appropriations _____

7. Fail to enforce a court order _____

8. Declare a law unconstitutional _____

9. Grant a reprieve _____

10. Replace some existing courts _____

11. Set free a person being held by the FBI _____

12. Propose an amendment _____

13. Confirm appointments _____

14. Ratify treaties _____

15. Declare the president's actions unconstitutional _____

Which branch of government do you think is the most powerful? Explain your answer.

_____

_____

_____

_____

FINDING YOUR WAY
THROUGH THE CONSTITUTION

PART A

Directions: The following quotations come from sections of the Constitution that no longer apply. After each quotation, write the amendment that changed the part of the Constitution being quoted. Explain in a sentence or two what the change was. For example, Article 1, Section 2, Paragraph 3 states, "Representatives . . . shall be apportioned among the several states . . . by adding to the whole numbers of free persons . . . three-fifths of all other persons." The three-fifths provision is now unconstitutional under the 13th and 14th Amendments, which outlawed slavery and gave freed slaves their rights.

1. "The Senate of the United States shall be composed of two Senators from each State, chosen by the Legislature. . . ."   Article 1, Section 3, Paragraph 1

   Overruled by: _____

   Explanation: _____

2. "The Congress shall assemble . . . on the first Monday in December. . . ."
          Article 1, Section 4, Paragraph 2

   Overruled by: _____

   Explanation: _____

3. "No Capitation, or other direct, Tax shall be laid. . . ."   Article 1, Section 9,
          Paragraph 4

   Overruled by: _____

   Explanation: _____

   _____

4. "The Person having the greatest Number of Votes shall be the President . . . if there be more than one who have such Majority, and have an equal Number of Votes, then the House of Representatives shall immediately chuse by Ballot one of them for President; and if no Person have a Majority, then from the five highest on the List. . . ."   Article II, Section 1, Paragraph 3

   Overruled by: _____

   Explanation: _____

   _____

5. "The judicial Power shall extend to all Cases . . . arising under this Constitution . . . to Controversies between two or more States; between a State and Citizens of another State. . . ."   Article III, Section 2, Paragraph 1

   Overruled by: _____

   Explanation: _____

Directions: Write down the number of the article, section, and paragraph where you would find information about the following items:

1. How Congress records its proceedings

   _____

2. Ratification of the Constitution

   _____

3. Court cases in federal jurisdiction

   _____

4. Admission of new states into the Union

   _____

5. The president's oath of office

   _____

6. Amending the Constitution

   _____

7. The Supremacy Clause

   _____

CONSTITUTIONAL CROSSWORD

Directions: Use the clues listed below to solve the crossword puzzle.

ACROSS

1. Congress has the power to punish this on the high seas.
3. Congress can fix the standard for _____ and measures.
5. These people formally elect the president.
7. This tax was outlawed by the 24th Amendment.
10. The right to vote
12. A high crime against the nation
13. A kind of trial covered by the Seventh Amendment
15. "in order to form a more perfect _____ . . ."
16. An impartial _____ is guaranteed in criminal cases.
17. This kind of "bill" is unconstitutional.
18. What bills might become
19. The president's branch

DOWN

2. The president is the commander in _____ of the armed forces.
3. Congress has the power to declare this.
4. The 21st Amendment eliminated this.
5. Paragraph 18 of the powers of Congress (two words)
6. "do _____ and establish this Constitution . . ."
8. The president's "stamp of disapproval"
9. This kind of corruption was outlawed in Article 3, Section 3.
11. Nickname for the 20th Amendment
14. One goal of the Constitution was to establish this.

INTERPRETING THE BILL OF RIGHTS

Directions: The situations listed below are *not* allowed by the Bill of Rights. Read each situation and then write down the number of the amendment that prohibits the action.

1. _____ Luke was found innocent of armed robbery, but the state decided to bring him to trial again anyway.

2. _____ After being found guilty of driving while intoxicated, the court ordered that Carolyn spend the next 30 years in solitary confinement.

3. _____ The citizens of Upper Creek voted to double the taxes of all Catholics.

4. _____ In a civil trial where the dispute was more than $20, both sides were denied a jury trial.

5. _____ For no apparent reason, the police stopped Rita while she was driving and began to search through her car trunk and personal luggage.

6. _____ The United States attorney general ordered all American citizens to turn in their rifles and pistols by noon on Saturday.

7. _____ Judge M.T. Nasty ordered a doctor to cut off the right hand of Marty, a convicted pickpocket.

8. _____ The federal government decided that state governments were no longer necessary.

9. _____ The president declared that the only rights Americans have are those listed in the first eight amendments.

10. _____ A United States representative prohibited a local newspaper from printing an editorial that was critical of her record.

11. _____ During peacetime the army ordered the residents of Seaville to house its soldiers.

12. _____ A group of labor leaders was told that it could not conduct a peaceful rally in the town square.

13. _____ Henry was arrested for shoplifting but was not brought to trial for five years.

14. _____ The judge insisted that the defendant take the stand and explain his actions on the night of the alleged crime.

15. _____ The police decided to place a "bug" in Kevin's home telephone in the hope that they would uncover some kind of crime.

16. _____ Congress passed a law banning the practice of Buddhism in the United States.

17. _____ Congress told the state of Montana that it would no longer be able to issue marriage licenses.

18. _____ Melissa was arrested and placed in jail without being informed of the nature or cause of the accusation.

19. _____ After being charged with arson, Nathaniel was denied the right of counsel for his defense.

20. _____ Judge Stone placed Kyle's bail for cheating on a high school exam at $500,000.

CLASSIFYING AMENDMENTS

PART A

Directions: Listed below are several amendment numbers. Next to each one, write its primary purpose. That purpose can be *voting rights, criminal rights, personal rights* (rights that protect people in their private lives), or *structural changes* (any changes made to solve a problem in the organization of government). For example, you would label the First Amendment *personal rights* because it protects free speech, press, religion, assembly, and petition.

A. Amendment 2 _____

B. Amendment 3 _____

C. Amendment 5 _____

D. Amendment 6 _____

E. Amendment 8 _____

F. Amendment 12 _____

G. Amendment 13 _____

H. Amendment 14 _____

I. Amendment 15 _____

J. Amendment 17 _____

K. Amendment 19 _____

L. Amendment 20 _____

M. Amendment 22 _____

N. Amendment 23 _____

O. Amendment 26 _____

PART B

WRITING AN ESSAY

Directions: Choose the one right or freedom in the Bill of Rights that you think is the most important. Write a short essay defending your selection.

_____

_____

_____

CONSTITUTIONAL NUMBERS

Directions: Match the phrase in the right-hand column with its correct number in the left-hand column by placing the appropriate letter in the space provided.

_____ 4   a. Minimum dollar value of property dispute that guarantees the right to a trial by jury

_____ 12   b. Number of years a representative must have been a citizen

_____ 35   c. The minimum number of presidential electors from any state

_____ 2   d. This amendment gave women the right to vote

_____ 435   e. Total number of United States senators

_____ 7   f. The number of representatives in the House

_____ 14   g. Total electoral college vote

_____ 26   h. The term of office for the president (in years)

_____ 7   f. The number of representatives in the House

_____ 14   g. Total electoral college vote

_____ 27   h. The term of office for the president (in years)

_____ 6   i. The maximum number of years any president can serve

_____ 10   j. This amendment outlaws cruel and unusual punishment

_____ 538   n. Number of years a senator must have been a citizen

_____ 25   o. Minimum number of representatives any state can have

_____ 8   p. Amendment that freed the slaves

_____ 1   q. The minimum age to be president

_____ 100   r. The term of office for a senator (in years)

_____ 9   s. Amendment that changed the way we elect the president

_____ 19   t. Number of years a candidate for president must have been a resident within the United States

THE FEDERALIST PAPERS SELECTIONS

When the delegates to the Constitutional Convention left Philadelphia in September of 1787, they were not sure whether or not the Constitution would be ratified by the necessary nine states. Delaware was the first state to ratify the Constitution on December 7, 1787. But ratification by the large states of Massachusetts, Pennsylvania, Virginia, and New York was needed to ensure the success of the new Constitution. Massachusetts and Pennsylvania ratified quickly. Virginia and New York, however, held out. The fight for ratification was especially fierce in New York.

One of the arenas where the battle for ratification was fought was newspapers. Under the imaginary name of Publius, James Madison, Alexander Hamilton, and John Jay wrote a series of essays that appeared on a regular basis in four out of five newspapers in New York City. No one knew who the real authors were. The essays, called *The Federalist,* explained the reasoning behind the new Constitution. There were 85 essays in all. The essays were later published in two volumes.

In this part of *The Constitution: Past, Present, and Future* you will find five *Federalist* essays. While you are reading the essays, it will be helpful to use your historical imagination. The language of the essays is quite difficult, but with a little work you will be able to understand them. The numbers in the left margin indicate the paragraph number. A good way to study the essays is with a partner or in a group. Read and study one sentence or paragraph at a time, using a dictionary to look up the unfamiliar words. At the beginning of each essay is an introduction explaining the most important points. At the end of each essay you will find review questions. And at the end of all five essays, you will find an activity that shows you how to make an outline that will help you study the essays in depth.

FEDERALIST 10

James Madison believed that the greatest threat to any republic comes from factions. Factions are groups of citizens driven by emotions or by self-interest, not by civic virtue. They try to violate the rights of other citizens or make the government do things that are harmful to the community. Can factions be abolished? Madison said that it would be difficult to abolish them. He thought, however, that the danger they posed could be controlled in a way that left liberties secure.

Madison's solution had two parts. First, the members of the legislature must be elected representatives. Second, the country and its population must be large and diverse, which means it must include people from many different backgrounds. People from many different backgrounds will have a variety of interests. Many small factions would not be as dangerous as a few larger ones. These two parts worked together. Madison believed that under the right conditions people would tend to elect people more virtuous than themselves. Even if they did not, the size and diversity of the country and its population would make the representatives diverse. Because of this diversity, no single faction would be able to gain the upper hand in the legislature. In part *Federalist* 10 was a reply to people who argued that size and diversity of population were bad for republics. As you can see, Madison thought factions were not bad, but good. In fact he thought they were necessary.

The Federalist No. 10: MADISON

November 22, 1787

To the People of the State of New York.

Among the numerous advantages promised by a well constructed Union, none deserves to be more accurately developed than its tendency to break and control the violence of faction. The friend of popular governments, never finds himself so much alarmed for their character and fate, as when he contemplates their propensity to this dangerous vice. He will not fail therefore to set a due value on any plan which, without violating the principles to which he is attached, provides a proper cure for it.

1 The instability, injustice and confusion introduced into the public councils, have in truth been the mortal diseases under which popular governments have every where perished; as they continue to be the favorite and fruitful topics from which the adversaries to liberty derive their most specious declamations. The valuable improvements made by the American Constitutions on the popular models, both ancient and modern, cannot certainly be too much admired; but it would be an unwarrantable partiality, to contend that they have as effectually obviated the danger on this side as was wished and expected. Complaints are every where heard from our most considerate and virtuous citizens, equally the friends of public and private faith, and of public and personal liberty; that our governments are too unstable; that the public good is disregarded in the conflicts of rival parties; and that measures are too often decided, not according to the rules of justice, and the rights of the minor party; but by the superior force of an interested and over-bearing majority. However anxiously we may wish that these complaints had no foundation, the evidence of known facts will not permit us to deny that they are in some degree true. It will be found indeed, on a candid review of our situation, that some of the distresses under which we labor, have been erroneously charged on the operation of our governments; but it will be found, at the same time, that other causes will not alone account for many of our heaviest misfortunes; and particularly, for that prevailing and increasing distrust of public engagements, and alarm for private rights, which are echoed from one end of the continent to the other. These must be chiefly, if not wholly, effects of the unsteadiness and injustice, with which a factious spirit has tainted our public administrations.

2 By a faction I understand a number of citizens, whether amounting to a majority or minority of the whole, who are united and actuated by some common impulse of passion, or of interest, adverse to the rights of other citizens, or to the permanent and aggregate interests of the community.

3 There are two methods of curing the mischiefs of faction: the one, by removing its causes; the other, by controling its effects.

4 There are again two methods of removing the causes of faction: the one by destroying the liberty which is essential to its existence; the other, by giving to every citizen the same opinions, the same passions, and the same interests.

5 It could never be more truly said than of the first remedy, that it is worse than the disease. Liberty is to faction, what air is to fire, an aliment without which it instantly expires. But it could not be a less folly to abolish liberty, which is essential to political life, because it nourishes faction, than it would be to wish the annihilation of air, which is essential to animal life, because it imparts to fire its destructive agency.

6 The second expedient is as impracticable, as the first would be unwise. As long as the reason of man continues fallible, and he is at liberty to exercise it, different opinions will be formed. As long as the connection subsists between his reason and his self-love, his opinions and his passions will have a reciprocal influence on each other; and the former will be objects to which the latter will attach themselves. The diversity in the faculties of men from which the rights of property originate, is not less an insuperable obstacle to a

uniformity of interests. The protection of these faculties is the first object of Government. From the protection of different and unequal faculties of acquiring property, the possession of different degrees and kinds of property immediately results: and from the influence of these on the sentiments and views of the respective proprietors, ensues a division of the society into different interests and parties.

7   The latent causes of faction are thus sown in the nature of man; and we see them every where brought into different degrees of activity, according to the different circumstances of civil society. A zeal for different opinions concerning religion, concerning Government and many other points, as well of speculation as of practice; an attachment to different leaders ambitiously contending for pre-eminence and power; or to persons of other descriptions whose fortunes have been interesting to the human passions, have in turn divided mankind into parties, inflamed them with mutual animosity, and rendered them much more disposed to vex and oppress each other, than to co-operate for their common good. So strong is this propensity of mankind to fall into mutual animosities, that where no substantial occasion presents itself, the most frivolous and fanciful distinctions have been sufficient to kindle their unfriendly passions, and excite their most violent conflicts. But the most common and durable source of factions, has been the various and unequal distribution of property. Those who hold, and those who are without property, have ever formed distinct interests in society. Those who are creditors, and those who are debtors, fall under a like discrimination. A landed interest, a manufacturing interest, a mercantile interest, a monied interest, with many lesser interests, grow up of necessity in civilized nations, and divide them into different classes, actuated by different sentiments and views. The regulation of these various and interfering interests forms the principal task of modern Legislation, and involves the spirit of party and faction in the necessary and ordinary operations of Government.

8   No man is allowed to be a judge in his own cause; because his interest would certainly bias his judgment, and, not improbably, corrupt his integrity. With equal, nay with greater reason, a body of men, are unfit to be both judges and parties, at the same time, yet, what are many of the most important acts of legislation, but so many judicial determinations, not indeed concerning the rights of single persons, but concerning the rights of large bodies of citizens; and what are the different classes of legislators, but advocates and parties to the causes which they determine? Is a law proposed concerning private debts? It is a question to which the creditors are parties on one side, and the debtors on the other. Justice ought to hold the balance between them. Yet the parties are and must be themselves the judges; and the most numerous party, or, in other words, the most powerful faction must be expected to prevail. Shall domestic manufactures be encouraged, and in what degree, by restrictions on foreign manufactures? are questions which would be differently decided by the landed and the manufacturing classes; and probably by neither, with a sole regard to justice and the public good. The apportionment of taxes on the various descriptions of property, is an act which seems to require the most exact impartiality; yet, there is perhaps no legislative act in which greater opportunity and temptation are given to a predominant party, to trample on the rules of justice. Every shilling with which they over-burden the inferior number, is a shilling saved to their own pockets.

9   It is in vain to say, that enlightened statesmen will be able to adjust these clashing interests, and render them all subservient to the public good. Enlightened statesmen will not always be at the helm: Nor, in many cases, can such an adjustment be made at all, without taking into view indirect and remote considerations, which will rarely prevail over the immediate interest which one party may find in disregarding the rights of another, or the good of the whole.

10   The interference to which we are brought, is, that the *causes* of faction cannot be removed; and that relief is only to be sought in the means of controling its *effects*.

11   If a faction consists of less than a majority, relief is supplied by the republican principle, which enables the majority to defeat its sinister views by regular vote: It may clog the administration, it may convulse the society; but it will be unable to execute and mask

its violence under the forms of the Constitution. When a majority is included in a faction, the form of popular government on the other hand enables it to sacrifice to its ruling passion or interest, both the public good and the rights of other citizens. To secure the public good, and private rights, against the danger of such a faction, and at the same time to preserve the spirit and the form of popular government, is then the great object to which our enquiries are directed: Let me add that it is the great desideratum, by which alone this form of government can be rescued from the opprobrium under which it has so long labored, and be recommended to the esteem and adoption of mankind.

12   By what means is this object attainable? Evidently by one of two only. Either the existence of the same passion or interest in a majority at the same time, must be prevented; or the majority, having such co-existent passion or interest, must be rendered, by their number and local situation, unable to concert and carry into effect schemes of oppression. If the impulse and the opportunity be suffered to coincide, we well know that neither moral nor religious motives can be relied on as an adequate control. They are not found to be such on the injustice and violence of individuals, and lose their efficacy in proportion to the number combined together; that is, in proportion as their efficacy becomes needful.

13   From this view of the subject, it may be concluded, that a pure Democracy, by which I mean, a Society, consisting of a small number of citizens, who assemble and administer the Government in person, can admit of no cure for the mischiefs of faction. A common passion or interest will, in almost every case, be felt by a majority of the whole; a communication and concert results from the form of Government itself; and there is nothing to check the inducements to sacrifice the weaker party, or an obnoxious individual. Hence it is, that such Democracies have ever been spectacles of turbulence and contention; have ever been found incompatible with personal security, or the rights of property; and have in general been as short in their lives, as they have been violent in their deaths. Theoretic politicians, who have patronized this species of Government, have erroneously supposed, that by reducing mankind to a perfect equality in their political rights, they would, at the same time, be perfectly equalized and assimilated in their possessions, their opinions, and their passions.

14   A Republic, by which I mean a Government in which the scheme of representation takes place, opens a different prospect, and promises the cure for which we are seeking. Let us examine the points in which it varies from pure Democracy, and we shall comprehend both the nature of the cure, and the efficacy which it must derive from the Union.

15   The two great points of difference between a Democracy and a Republic are, first, the delegation of the Government, in the latter, to a small number of citizens elected by the rest: secondly, the greater number of citizens, and greater sphere of country, over which the latter may be extended.

16   The effect of the first difference is, on the one hand to refine and enlarge the public views, by passing them through the medium of a chosen body of citizens, whose wisdom may best discern the true interest of their country, and whose patriotism and love of justice, will be least likely to sacrifice it to temporary or partial considerations. Under such a regulation, it may well happen that the public voice pronounced by the representatives of the people, will be more consonant to the public good, than if pronounced by the people themselves convened for the purpose. On the other hand, the effect may be inverted. Men of factious tempers, of local prejudices, or of sinister designs, may by intrigue, by corruption or by other means, first obtain the suffrages, and then betray the interests of the people. The question resulting is, whether small or extensive Republics are most favorable to the election of proper guardians of the public weal: and it is clearly decided in favor of the latter by two obvious considerations.

17   In the first place it is to be remarked that however small the Republic may be, the Representatives must be raised to a certain number, in order to guard against the cabals of a few; and that however large it may be, they must be limited to a certain number, in order to guard against the confusion of a multitude. Hence the number of Representatives

40

in the two cases, not being in proportion to that of the Constituents, and being proportionally greatest in the small Republic, it follows, that if the proportion of fit characters, be not less, in the large than in the small Republic, the former will present a greater option, and consequently a greater probability of a fit choice.

18   In the next place, as each Representative will be chosen by a greater number of citizens in the large than in the small Republic, it will be more difficult for unworthy candidates to practise with success the vicious arts, by which elections are too often carried; and the suffrages of the people being more free, will be more likely to centre on men who possess the most attractive merit, and the most diffusive and established characters.

19   It must be confessed, that in this, as in most other cases, there is a mean, on both sides of which inconveniencies will be found to lie. By enlarging too much the number of electors, you render the representative too little acquainted with all their local circumstances and lesser interests; as by reducing it too much, you render him unduly attached to these, and too little fit to comprehend and pursue great and national objects. The Federal Constitution forms a happy combination in this respect; the great and aggregate interests being referred to the national, the local and particular, to the state legislatures.

20   The other point of difference is, the greater number of citizens and extent of territory which may be brought within the compass of Republican, than of Democratic Government; and it is this circumstance principally which renders factious combinations less to be dreaded than the former, than in the latter. The smaller the society, the fewer probably will be the distinct parties and interests composing it; the fewer the distinct parties and interests, the more frequently will a majority be found of the same party; and the smaller the number of individuals composing a majority, and the smaller the compass within which they are placed, the more easily will they concert and execute their plans of oppression. Extend the sphere, and you take in a greater variety of parties and interests; you make it less probable that a majority of the whole will have a common motive to invade the rights of other citizens; or if such a common motive exists, it will be more difficult for all who feel it to discover their own strength, and to act in unison with each other. Besides other impediments, it may be remarked, that where there is a consciousness of unjust or dishonorable purposes, communication is always checked by distrust, in proportion to the number whose concurrence is necessary.

21   Hence it clearly appears, that the same advantage, which a Republic has over a Democracy, in controling the effects of faction, is enjoyed by a large over a small Republic—is enjoyed by the Union over the States composing it. Does this advantage consist in the substitution of Representatives, whose enlightened views and virtuous sentiments render them superior to local prejudices, and to schemes of injustice? It will not be denied, that the Representation of the Union will be most likely to possess these requisite endowments. Does it consist in the greater security afforded by a greater variety of parties, against the event of any one party being able to outnumber and oppress the rest? In an equal degree does the encreased variety of parties, comprised within the Union, encrease this security. Does it, in fine, consist in the greater obstacles opposed to the concert and accomplishment of the secret wishes of an unjust and interested majority? Here, again, the extent of the Union gives it the most palpable advantage.

22   The influence of factious leaders may kindle a flame within their particular States, but will be unable to spread a general conflagration through the other States: a religious sect, may degenerate into a political faction in a part of the Confederacy; but the variety of sects dispersed over the entire face of it, must secure the national Councils against any danger from that source: a rage for paper money, for an abolition of debts, for an equal division of property, or for any other improper or wicked project, will be less apt to prevade the whole body of the Union, than a particular member of it; in the same proportion as such a malady is more likely to taint a particular county or district, than an entire State.

In the extent and proper structure of the Union, therefore, we behold a Republican remedy for the diseases most incident to Republican Government. And according to the

23   degree of pleasure and pride, we feel in being Republicans, ought to be our zeal in cherishing the spirit, and supporting the character of Federalists.

PUBLIUS.

REVIEWING THE MAIN IDEAS

1. Madison states that factions can include either a minority or a majority of the population. Yet he does not think that minority factions are as dangerous as majority factions. Study paragraph 11, and then explain why he feels minority factions are not as dangerous as majority factions.
2. Madison describes two different ways of abolishing factions and rejects them both. Study paragraphs 4 and 5. What is the first way of abolishing factions? Why does Madison reject it?
3. In paragraph 7 Madison says that factions can have many causes. What cause does Madison say is the most common cause?
4. In paragraphs 17-19 Madison gives a number of reasons that virtuous representatives are more likely to be elected from large districts than from small districts. State at least one of the reasons.
5. Do you think factions are good or bad? Support your view.

FEDERALIST 51

Many of the Antifederalists (people who opposed the Constitution) did so because they thought that it violated the principle of separation of powers. This argument may surprise you. After all, the Constitution divides the government into three branches: a legislative branch to make the laws, an executive branch to carry out the laws, and a judicial branch to interpret the laws. But, as the Antifederalists explained, this was not the whole story. Why not? Because the Constitution also provides ways for one branch to check, or limit, another. Can you see why checks might be viewed as violations of the principle of separation of powers? When the president vetoes a law, isn't he or she taking a part in legislative work? When the Senate holds a trial of impeachment, isn't it taking a part in judicial work? When the Senate confirms a presidential appointment, isn't it taking a part in executive work?

The purpose of *Federalist* 51 was to give a different explanation of separation of powers, one that showed why checks were needed. In this essay Madison admitted that checks violated the principle of separation of powers. He said, however, that these small violations were necessary to prevent even greater violations.

The Federalist No. 51: MADISON

February 6, 1788

To the People of the State of New York.

1   To what expedient then shall we finally resort for maintaining in practice the necessary partition of power among the several departments, as laid down in the constitution. The only answer that can be given is, that as all these exterior provisions are found to be inadequate, the defect must be supplied, by so contriving the interior structure of the government, as that its several constituent parts may, by their mutual relations, be the means of keeping each other in their proper places. Without presuming to undertake a full developement of this important idea, I will hazard a few general observations, which may perhaps place it in a clearer light, and enable us to form a more correct judgment of the principles and structure of the government planned by the convention.

2   In order to lay a due foundation for that separate and distinct exercise of the different powers of government, which to a certain extent, is admitted on all hands to be essential to the preservation of liberty, it is evident that each department should have a will of its own; and consequently should be so constituted, that the members of each should have as

little agency as possible in the appointment of the members of the others. Were this principle rigorously adhered to, it would require that all the appointments for the supreme executive, legislative, and judiciary magistracies, should be drawn from the same fountain of authority, the people, through channels, having no communication whatever with one another. Perhaps such a plan of constructing the several departments would be less difficult in practice than it may in contemplation appear. Some difficulties however, and some additional expence, would attend the execution of it. Some deviations therefore from the principle must be admitted. In the constitution of the judiciary department in particular, it might be inexpedient to insist rigorously on the principle; first, because peculiar qualifications being essential in the members, the primary consideration ought to be to select that mode of choice, which best secures these qualifications; secondly, because the permanent tenure by which the appointments are held in that department, must soon destroy all sense of dependence on the authority conferring them.

3   It is equally evident that the members of each department should be as little dependent as possible on those of the others, for the emoluments annexed to their offices. Were the executive magistrate, or the judges, not independent of the legislature in this particular, their independence in every other would be merely nominal.

4   But the great security against a gradual concentration of the several powers in the same department, consists in giving to those who administer each department, the necessary constitutional means, and personal motives, to resist encroachments of the others. The provision for defence must in this, as in all other cases, be made commensurate to the danger of attack. Ambition must be made to counteract ambition. The interest of the man must be connected with the constitutional rights of the place. It may be a reflection on human nature, that such devices should be necessary to controul the abuses of government. But what is government itself but the greatest of all reflections on human nature? If men were angels, no government would be necessary. If angels were to govern men, neither external nor internal countrouls on government would be necessary. In framing a government which is to be administered by men over men, the great difficulty lies in this: You must first enable the government to controul the governed; and in the next place, oblige it to controul itself. A dependence on the people is no doubt the primary controul on the government; but experience has taught mankind the necessity of auxiliary precautions.

5   This policy of supplying by opposite and rival interests, the defect of better motives, might be traced through the whole system of human affairs, private as well as public. We see it particularly displayed in all the subordinate distributions of power; where the constant aim is to divide and arrange the several offices in such a manner as that each may be a check on the other; that the private interest of every individual, may be a centinel over the public rights. These inventions of prudence cannot be less requisite in the distribution of the supreme powers of the state.

6   But it is not possible to give to each department an equal power of self defence. In republican government the legislative authority, necessarily, predominates. The remedy for this inconveniency is, to divide the legislature into different branches; and to render them by different modes of election, and different principles of action, as little connected with each other, as the nature of their common functions, and their common dependence on the society, will admit. It may even be necessary to guard against dangerous encroachments by still further precautions. As the weight of the legislative authority requires that it should be thus divided, the weakness of the executive may require, on the other hand, that it should be fortified. An absolute negative, on the legislature, appears at first view to be the natural defence with which the executive magistrate should be armed. But perhaps it would be neither altogether safe, nor alone sufficient. On ordinary occasions, it might not be exerted with the requisite firmness; and on extraordinary occasions, it might be perfidiously abused. May not this defect of an absolute negative be supplied, by some qualified connection between this weaker department, and the weaker branch of the stronger department, by which the latter may be led to support the constitutional rights of

the former, without being too much detached from the rights of its own department?

7   If the principles on which these observations are founded be just, as I persuade myself they are, and they be applied as a criterion, to the several state constitutions, and to the federal constitution, it will be found, that if the latter does not perfectly correspond with them, the former are infinitely less able to bear such a test.

8   There are moreover two considerations particularly applicable to the federal system of America, which place that system in a very interesting point of view.

First. In a single republic, all the power surrendered by the people, is submitted to the administration of a single government; and usurpations are guarded against by a division of the government into distinct and separate departments. In the compound republic of

9 America, the power surrendered by the people is first divided between two distinct governments, and then the portion allotted to each, subdivided among distinct and separate departments. Hence a double security arises to the rights of the people. The different governments will controul each other; at the same time that each will be controuled by itself.

Second. It is of great importance in a republic, not only to guard the society against the

10 oppression of its rulers; but to guard one part of society against the injustice of the other part. Different interests necessarily exist in different classes of citizens. If a majority be united by a common interest, the rights of the minority will be insecure. There are but two methods of providing against this evil: The one by creating a will in the community independent of the majority, that is, of the society itself; the other by comprehending in the society so many separate descriptions of citizens, as will render an unjust combination of a majority of the whole, very improbable, if not impracticable. The first method prevails in all governments possessing an hereditary or self appointed authority. This at best is but a precarious security; because a power independent of the society may as well espouse the unjust views of the major, as the rightful interests, of the minor party, and may possibly be turned against both parties. The second method will be exemplified in the federal republic of the United States. Whilst all authority in it will be derived from and dependent on the society, the society itself will be broken into so many parts, interests and classes of citizens, that the rights of individuals or of the minority, will be in little danger from interested combinations of the majority. In a free government, the security for civil rights must be the same as for religious rights. It consists in the one case in the multiplicity of interests, and in the other, in the multiplicity of sects. The degree of security in both cases will depend on the number of interests and sects; and this may be presumed to depend on the extent of country and number of people comprehended under the same government. This view of the subject must particularly recommend a proper federal system to all the sincere and considerate friends of republican government: Since it shews that in exact proportion as the territory of the union may be formed into more circumscribed confederacies or states, oppressive combinations of a majority will be facilitated, the best security under the republican form, for the rights of every class of citizens, will be diminished; and consequently, the stability and independence of some member of the government, the only other security, must be proportionally increased. Justice is the end of government. It is the end of civil society. It ever has been, and ever will be pursued, until it be obtained, or until liberty be lost in the pursuit. In a society under the forms of which the stronger faction can readily unite and oppress the weaker, anarchy may as truly be said to reign, as in a state of nature where the weaker individual is not secured against the violence of the stronger: And as in the latter state even the stronger individuals are prompted by the uncertainty of their condition, to submit to a government which may protect the weak as well as themselves: So in the former state, will the more powerful factions or parties be gradually induced by a like motive, to wish for a government which will protect all parties, the weaker as well as the more powerful. It can be little doubted, that if the state of Rhode Island was separated from the confederacy, and left to itself, the insecurity of rights under the popular form of government within such narrow limits, would be displayed by such reiterated oppressions

44

of factious majorities, that some power altogether independent of the people would soon be called for by the voice of the very factions whose misrule had proved the necessity of it. In the extended republic of the United States, and among the great variety of interests, parties and sects which it embraces, a coalition of a majority of the whole society could seldom take place on any other principles than those of justice and the general good; and there being thus less danger to a minor from the will of the major party, there must be less pretext also, to provide for the security of the former, by introducing into the government a will not dependent on the latter; or in other words, a will independent of the society itself. It is no less certain than it is important, notwithstanding the contrary opinions which have been entertained, that the larger the society, provided it lie within a practicable sphere, the more duly capable it will be of self government. And happily for the *republican cause,* the practicable sphere may be carried to a very great extent, by a judicious modification and mixture of the *federal principle.*

PUBLIUS.

REVIEWING THE MAIN IDEAS

1. In paragraph 6 Madison says that it isn't possible to give each branch of government equal powers of self-defense against the others, because one of the the branches will always be the strongest. Which branch does Madison say is the strongest? Why?
2. Also in paragraph 6 Madison gives a remedy for this problem. What is the remedy?
3. Madison compares the separation and competition between the three branches of the national government to two other things. Study paragraphs 9 and 10, and then state at least one of the things that Madison uses as a comparison.
4. If you could add a fourth branch of government, what would it be? Why? What would the duties of the fourth branch be?

EXCERPTS FROM FEDERALIST 62 and 63

The most important part of *Federalist* 62 and *Federalist* 63 is a long discussion of a single question: "Why is the Senate so small, and why is its term of office so long?" Madison began this discussion midway through *Federalist* 62 and ends it midway through *Federalist* 63. These excerpts provide the entire discussion.

Why was the question important? Many Antifederalists saw danger in the small size of the Senate and its long term of office. Combined with the other features of the Senate, such as the tougher requirements for membership and the selection of senators by state legislatures, they thought the small size and long term were more dangerous still. The Antifederalists believed that the Senate was very likely to turn into an aristocratic governing body much like the House of Lords in the English Parliament. They suspected that this was just what the delegates to the Constitutional Convention wanted. This suspicion was one of the reasons that they considered the Constitution an undemocratic plot.

Federalist 62 and 63 were an important part of Madison's reply to those who held such suspicions. Madison never denied that there was something undemocratic about the Senate. He argued, however, that representative democracies have certain dangerous flaws that the existence of the Senate will correct. In the long run this supposedly undemocratic part of the government would help the representative democracy thrive.

Note to the reader: As you read you will notice the term *national character.* It is important to remember that the English language has changed since the 1700s. The term as Madison used it referred to the nation's reputation (what other governments thought of it), and not to its spirit or personality.

From The Federalist No. 62: MADISON

February 27, 1788

To the People of the State of New York.

1   IV. The number of senators and the duration of their appointment come next to be considered. In order to form an accurate judgment on both these points, it will be proper to enquire into the purposes which are to be answered by a senate; and in order to ascertain these it will be necessary to review the inconveniencies which a republic must suffer from the want of such an institution.

2   *First.* It is a misfortune incident to republican government, though in a less degree than to other governments, that those who administer it, may forget their obligations to their constituents, and prove unfaithful to their important trust. In this point of view, a senate, as a second branch of the legislative assembly, distinct from, and dividing the power with, a first, must be in all cases a salutary check on the government. It doubles the security to the people, by requiring the concurrence of two distinct bodies in schemes of usurpation or perfidy, where the ambition or corruption of one, would otherwise be sufficient. This is a precaution founded on such clear principles, and now so well understood in the United States, that it would be more than superfluous to enlarge on it. I will barely remark that as the improbability of sinister combinations will be in proportion to the dissimilarity in the genius of the two bodies; it must be politic to distinguish them from each other by every circumstance which will consist with a due harmony in all proper measures, and with the genuine principles of republican government.

3   *Secondly.* The necessity of a senate is not less indicated by the propensity of all single and numerous assemblies, to yield to the impulse of sudden and violent passions, and to be seduced by factious leaders, into intemperate and pernicious resolutions. Examples on this subject might be cited without number; and from proceedings within the United States, as well as from the history of other nations. But a position that will not be contradicted need not be proved. All that need be remarked is that a body which is to correct this infirmity ought itself be free from it, and consequently ought to be less numerous. It ought moreover to possess great firmness, and consequently ought to hold its authority by a tenure of considerable duration.

4   *Thirdly.* Another defect to be supplied by a senate lies in a want of due acquaintance with the objects and principles of legislation. It is not possible that an assembly of men called for the most part from pursuits of a private nature, continued in appointment for a short time, and led by no permanent motive to devote the intervals of public occupation to a study of the laws, the affairs and the comprehensive interests of their country, should, if left wholly to themselves, escape a variety of important errors in the exercise of their legislative trust. It may be affirmed, on the best grounds, that no small share of the present embarrassments of America is to be charged on the blunders of our governments; and that these have proceeded from the heads rather than the hearts of most of the authors of them. What indeed are all the repealing, explaining and amending laws, which fill and disgrace our voluminous codes, but so many monuments of deficient wisdom; so many impeachments exhibited by each succeeding, against each preceding session; so many admonitions to the people of the value of those aids which may be expected from a well constituted senate?

5   A good government implies two things; first, fidelity to the object of government, which is the happiness of the people; secondly, a knowledge of the means by which that object can be best attained. Some governments are deficient in both these qualities: Most governments are deficient in the first. I scruple not to assert that in the American governments, too little attention has been paid to the last. The federal constitution avoids this error; and what merits particular notice, it provides for the last in a mode which increases the security for the first.

6   *Fourthly.* The mutability in the public councils, arising from a rapid succession of new members, however qualified they may be, points out in the strongest manner, the necessity of some stable institution in the government. Every new election in the states, is

found to change one half of the representatives. From this change of men must proceed a change of opinions; and from a change of opinions, a change of measures. But a continual change even of good measures is inconsistent with every rule of prudence, and every prospect of success. The remark is verified in private life, and become more just as well as more important, in national transactions.

7   To trace the mischievous effects of a mutable government would fill a volume. I will hint a few only, each of which will be perceived to be a source of innumerable others.

In the first place it forfeits the respect and confidence of other nations, and all the advantages connected with national character. An individual who is observed to be inconstant to his plans, or perhaps to carry on his affairs without any plan at all, is marked at once by all prudent people as a speedy victim to his own unsteadiness and folly. His more friendly neighbours may pity him; but all will decline to connect their fortunes with his; and not a few will seize the opportunity of making their fortunes out of his. One nation is

8   to another what one individual is to another; with this melancholy distinction perhaps, that the former with fewer of the benevolent emotions than the latter, are under fewer restraints also from taking undue advantage of the indiscretions of each other. Every nation consequently whose affairs betray want of wisdom and stability, may calculate on every loss which can be sustained from the more systematic policy of its wiser neighbours.

But the best instruction on this subject is unhappily conveyed to America by the example of her own situation. She finds that she is held in no respect by her friends; that she is the derision of her enemies; and that she is prey to every nation which has an interest in speculating on her fluctuating councils and embarrassed affairs.

The internal effects of a mutable policy are still more calamitous. It poisons the blessings of liberty itself. It will be of little avail to the people that the laws are made by men of their own choice, if the laws be so voluminous that they cannot be read, or so

9   incoherent that they cannot be understood; if they be repealed or revised before they are promulged, or undergo such incessant changes that no man who knows what the law is to-day can guess what it will be to-morrow. Law is defined to be a rule of action; but how can that be a rule, which is little known and less fixed?

Another effect of public instablility is the unreasonable advantage it gives to the sagacious, the enterprising and the moneyed few, over the industrious and uninformed mass of people. Every new regulation concerning commerce or revenue, or in any manner affecting the value of the different species of property, presents a new harvest to those who watch the change, and can trace its consequences; a harvest reared not by them-

10   selves but by the toils and cares of the great body of their fellow citizens. This is a state of things in which it may be said with some truth that laws are made for the *few* not for the *many*.

In another point of view great injury results from an unstable government. The want of confidence in the public councils damps every useful undertaking; the success and profit of which may depend on a continuance of existing arrangements. What prudent merchant will hazard his fortunes in any new branch of commerce, when he knows not but that his plans may be rendered unlawful before they can be executed? What farmer or manufac-

11   turer will lay himself out for the encouragement given to any particular cultivation or establishment, when he can have not assurance that his preparatory labors and advances will not render him a victim to an inconstant government? In a word no great improvement or laudable enterprise, can go forward, which requires the auspices of a steady system of national policy.

But the most deplorable effect of all is that diminution of attachment and reverence which steals into the hearts of the people, towards a political system which betrays so

12   many marks of infirmity, and disappoints so many of their flattering hopes. No government any more than an individual will long be respected, without being truly respectable, nor be truly respectable without possessing a certain portion of order and stability.

PUBLIUS.

From The Federalist No. 63: MADISON

To the People of the State of New York.   March 1, 1788

1 A fifth desideratum illustrating the utility of a Senate, is the want of a due sense of national character. Without a select and stable member of the government, the esteem of foreign powers will not only be forfeited by an unenlightened and variable policy, proceeding from the causes already mentioned; but the national councils will not possess that sensibility to the opinion of the world, which is perhaps not less necessary in order to merit, than it is to obtain, its respect and confidence.

2 An attention to the judgment of other nations is important to every government for two reasons: The one is, that independently of the merits of any particular plan or measure, it is desireable on various accounts, that it should appear to other nations as the offspring of a wise and honorable policy: The second is, that in doubtful cases, particularly where the national councils may be warped by some strong passion, or momentary interest, the presumed or known opinion of the impartial world, may be the best guide that can be followed. What has not America lost by her want of character with foreign nations? And how many errors and follies would she not have avoided, if the justice and propriety of her measures had in every instance been previously tried by the light in which they would probably appear to the unbiassed part of mankind?

3 Yet however requisite a sense of national character may be, it is evident that it can never be sufficiently possessed by a numerous and changeable body. It can only be found in a number so small, that a sensible degree of the praise and blame of public measures may be the portion of each individual; or in an assembly so durably invested with public trust, that the pride and consequence of its members may be sensibly incorporated with the reputation and prosperity of the community. The half-yearly representatives of Rhode-Island, would probably have been little affected in their deliberations on the iniquitous measures of that state, by arguments drawn from the light in which such measures would be viewed by foreign nations, or even by the sister states; whilst it can scarcely be doubted, that if the concurrence of a select and stable body had been necessary, a regard to national character alone, would have prevented the calamities under which that misguided people is now laboring.

4 I add as a *sixth* defect, the want in some important cases of a due responsiblility in the government to the people, arising from that frequency of elections, which in other cases produces this responsibility. This remark will perhaps appear not only new but paradoxical. It must nevertheless be acknowledged, when explained, to be as undeniable as it is important.

5 Responsibility in order to be reasonable must be limited to objects within the power of the responsible party; and in order to be effectual, must relate to operations of that power, of which a ready and proper judgment can be formed by the constituents. The objects of government may be divided into two general classes; the one depending on measures which have singly an immediate and sensible operation; the other depending on a succession of well chosen and well connected measures, which have a gradual and perhaps unobserved operation. The importance of the latter description to the collective and permanent welfare of every country needs no explanation. And yet it is evident, that an assembly elected for so short a term as to be unable to provide more than one or two links in a chain of measures, on which the general welfare may essentially depend, ought not to be answerable for the final result, any more than a steward or tenant, engaged for one year, could be justly made to answer for places or improvements, which could not be accomplished in less than half a dozen years. Nor is it possible for the people to estimate the *share* of influence which their annual assemblies may respectively have on events resulting from the mixed transactions of several years. It is sufficiently difficult at any rate to preserve a personal responsibility in the members of a *numerous* body, for such acts of the body as have an immediate, detached and palpable operation on its constituents.

6   The proper remedy for this defect must be an additional body in the legislative department, which, having sufficient permanency to provide for such objects as require a continued attention, and a train of measures, may be justly and effectually answerable for the attainment of those objects.

  Thus far I have considered the circumstances which point out the necessity of a well constructed senate, only as they relate to the representatives of the people. To a people as little blinded by prejudice, or corrupted by flattery, as those whom I address, I shall not scruple to add, that such an institution may be sometimes necessary, as a defence to the people against their own temporary errors and delusions. As the cool and deliberate sense of the community ought in all governments, and actually will in all free governments ultimately prevail over the views of its rulers; so there are particular moments in

7 public affairs, when the people stimulated by some irregular passion, or some illicit advantage, or misled by the artful misrepresentations of interested men, may call for measures which they themselves will afterwards by the most ready to lament and condemn. In these critical moments, how salutary will be the interference of some temperate and respectable body of citizens, in order to check the misguided career, and to suspend the blow meditated by the people against themselves, until reason, justice and truth, can regain their authority over the public mind? What bitter anguish would not the people of Athens have often escaped, if their government had contained so provident a safeguard against the tyranny of their own passions? Popular liberty might then have escaped the indelible reproach of decreeing to the same citizens, the hemlock on one day, and statues on the next. . . .

PUBLIUS.

REVIEWING THE MAIN IDEAS

1. Study *Federalist* 62, paragraphs 8-10 and *Federalist* 63, paragraphs 1-6. Madison gives six reasons for thinking that the small size and long term of office of the Senate are good things rather than bad things. For example, here is reason number four: Because the members of the House of Representatives will change so often, the House will make and change laws much too often. To correct this flaw the Senate must have a long term of office. List at least three of the other five reasons Madison gives.

2. Of these six reasons, Madison spends the most time talking about reason number four. In *Federalist* 62, paragraphs 8-12, he makes five separate points to show why frequent change in the laws is so terrible. For example, here is point number three: If the laws change too often ordinary people will not have time to figure them out. This will give an unfair advantage to rich people. List at least two of the other four points Madison makes.

3. Study *Federalist* 63, paragraph 7. Madison says that the Senate will give the American people a protection against themselves. Why does he think that the people need protection against themselves?

4. Of the six reasons Madison gives for thinking that the small size and long term of office of the Senate are good things, which reason do you think is the most important? Support your answer.

FEDERALIST 70

One of the sharpest differences between the Constitution and the Articles of Confederation was that the Constitution provided for a single strong president. Many Antifederalists feared that the president would be too strong. They said that the executive power should be "plural" instead of "unitary." (*Plural* means "more than one." *Unitary* means "of one unit.") This argument could have meant two things. One was that the power of the chief executive would be shared among several people instead of just one. Another was that the executive power would be given to just one person, but he could be overruled by an executive advisory council.

In *Federalist* 70 Alexander Hamilton argued against both of these ideas. He said that the executive power should be given to only one person and that no executive advisory council should be given the authority to overrule him. He made three related recommendations. One was that legislatures should act slowly but that executives should act swiftly (or, as he put it, with "energy"). Another was that plurality in the executive branch would keep it from acting swiftly. Finally, he said that plurality would keep the executive branch from being accountable to the people.

Note to the reader: You will notice that in paragraph 1 Hamilton used the Romans as an example to support his view that "energy in the executive is a leading character in the definition of good government." In doing so, he praised the Roman institution of the "dictator." It is important to realize that the English language has changed since Hamilton wrote this essay. Hamilton is not approving of dictatorship in the modern sense of the word. The dictator in the Roman Republic was a temporary official who was appointed to deal with emergencies such as a threat by enemy nations to the food supply. Although the dictator's power was unlimited in all matters relating to the emergency, in all other matters he was completely powerless. Moreover, his term of office ended in six months or when the crisis ended, whichever came first.

The Federalist No. 70: HAMILTON

March 15, 1788

To the People of the State of New York.

1 There is an idea, which is not without its advocates, that a vigorous executive is inconsistent with the genius of republican government. The enlightened well wishers to this species of government must at least hope that the supposition is destitute of foundation; since they can never admit its truth, without at the same time admitting condemnation of their own principles. Energy in the executive is a leading character in the definition of good government. It is essential to the protection of the community against foreign attacks: It is not less essential to the steady administration of laws, to the protection of property against those irregular and high handed combinations, which sometimes interrupt the ordinary course of justice, to the security of liberty against the enterprises and assaults of ambition, of faction and of anarchy. Every man the least conversant in Roman story knows how often that republic was obliged to take refuge in the absolute power of a single man, under the formidable title of dictator, as well against the intrigues of ambitious individuals, who aspired to the tyranny, and the seditions of whole classes of the community, whose conduct threatened the existence of all government, as against the invasions of external enemies, who menaced the conquest and destruction of Rome.

2 There can be no need however to multiply arguments or examples on this head. A feeble executive implies a feeble execution of the government. A feeble execution is but another phrase for a bad execution; And a government ill executed, whatever it may be in theory, must be in practice a bad government.

3 Taking it for granted, therefore, that all men of sense will agree in the necessity of an energetic executive; it will only remain to inquire, what are the ingredients which constitute this energy—how far can they be combined with those other ingredients which constitute safety in the republican sense? And how far does this combination characterize the plan, which has been reported by the convention?

4 The ingredients, which constitute energy in the executive, are first unity, secondly duration, thirdly an adequate provision for its support, fourthly competent powers.

50

The circumstances which constitute safety in the republican sense are, 1st. a due

5   dependence on the people, secondly a due responsibility.

Those politicians and statesmen, who have been the most celebrated for the sound-
ness of their principles, and for the justness of their views, have declared in favor of a

6   single executive and a numerous legislature. They have with great propriety considered
energy as the most necessary qualification of the former, and have regarded this as most
applicable to power in a single hand; while they have with equal propriety considered the
latter as best adapted to deliberation and wisdom, and best calculated to conciliate the
confidence of the people and to secure their privileges and interests.

That unity is conducive to energy will not be disputed. Decision, activity, secrecy, and

7   dispatch will generally characterise the proceedings of one man, in a much more eminent
degree, than the proceedings of any greater number; and in proportion as the number is
increased, these qualities will be diminished.

This unity may be destroyed in two ways; either by vesting the power in two or more
magistrates of equal dignity and authority; or by vesting it ostensibly in one man, subject
in whole or in part to the controul and co-operation of others, in the capacity of counsellors to him. Of the first the two consuls of Rome may serve as an example; of the last we

8   shall find examples in the constitutions of several of the states. New-York and New-
Jersey, if I recollect right, are the only states, which have entrusted the executive authority wholly to single men.[1] Both these methods of destroying the unity of the executive
have their partisans; but the votaries of an executive council are the most numerous. They
are both liable, if not to equal, to similar objections; and may in most lights be examined
in conjunction.

The experience of other nations will afford little instruction on this head. As far
however as it teaches any thing, it teaches us not to be inamoured of plurality in the
executive. We have seen that the Achæans on an experiment of two Prætors, were
induced to abolish one. The Roman history records many instances of mischiefs to the
republic from the dissentions between the consuls, and between the military tribunes,
who were at times substituted to the consuls. But it gives us no specimens of any peculiar
advantages derived to the state, from the circumstance of the plurality of those magistrates. That the dissentions between them were not more frequent, or more fatal, is
matter of astonishment; until we advert to the singular position in which the republic was

9   almost continually placed and to the prudent policy pointed out by the circumstances of
the state, and pursued by the consuls, of making a division of the government between
them. The Patricians engaged in a perpetual struggle with the Plebians for the preservation of their antient authorities and dignities; the consuls, who were generally chosen out
of the former body, were commonly united by the personal interest they had in the
defence of the privileges of their order. In addition to this motive of union, after the arms
of the republic had considerably expanded the bounds of its empire, it became an established custom with the consuls to divide the administration between themselves by lot;
one of them remaining at Rome to govern the city and its environs; the other taking the
command in the more distant provinces. This expedient must no doubt have had great
influence in preventing those collisions and rivalships, which might otherwise have em-
broiled the peace of the republic.

But quitting the dim light of historical research, and attaching ourselves purely to the

10   dictates of reason and good sense, we shall discover much greater cause to reject than to
approve the idea of plurality in the executive, under any modification whatever.

Wherever two or more persons are engaged in any common enterprise or pursuit, there
is always danger of difference of opinion. If it be a public trust or office in which they are
cloathed with equal dignity and authority, there is peculiar danger of personal emulation

---

[1] *New-York has no council except for the single purpose of appointing to offices; New-
Jersey has a council, whom the governor may consult. But I think from the terms of the
constitution their resolutions do not bind him.* (Publius)

11 and even animosity. From either and especially from all these causes, the most bitter dissentions are apt to spring. Whenever these happen, they lessen the respectability, weaken the authority, and distract the plans and operations of those whom they divide. If they should unfortunately assail the supreme executive magistracy of a country, consisting of a plurality of persons, they might impede or frustrate the most important measures of the government, in the most critical emergencies of the state. And what is still worse, they might split the community into the most violent and irreconcilable factions, adhering differently to the different individuals who composed the magistracy.

12 Men often oppose a thing merely because they have had no agency in planning it, or because it may have been planned by those whom they dislike. But if they have been consulted and have happened to disapprove, opposition then becomes in their estimation an indispensable duty of self love. They seem to think themselves bound in honor, and by all the motives of personal infallibility to defeat the success of what has been resolved upon, contrary to their sentiments. Men of upright, benevolent tempers have too many opportunities of remarking with horror, to what desperate lengths this disposition is sometimes carried, and how often the great interests of society are sacrificed to the vanity, to the conceit and to the obstinacy of individuals, who have credit enough to make their passions and their caprices interesting to mankind. Perhaps the question now before the public may in its consequences afford melancholy proofs of the effects of this despicable frailty, or rather detestable vice in the human character.

13 Upon the principles of a free government, inconveniencies from the source just mentioned must necessarily be submitted to in the formation of the legislature; but it is unnecessary and therefore unwise to introduce them into the constitution of the executive. It is here too that they may be most pernicious. In the legislature, promptitude of decision is oftener an evil than a benefit. The differences of opinion, and the jarrings of parties in that department of the government, though they may sometimes obstruct salutary plans, yet often promote deliberation and circumspection; and serve to check excesses in the majority. When a resolution too is once taken, the opposition must be at an end. That resolution is a law, and resistance to it punishable. But no favourable circumstances palliate or atone for the disadvantages of dissention in the executive department. Here they are pure and unmixed. There is no point at which they cease to operate. They serve to embarrass and weaken the execution of the plan or measure, to which they relate, from the first step to the final conclusion of it. They constantly counteract those qualities in the executive, which are the most necessary ingredients in its composition, vigour and expedition, and this without any counterballancing good. In the conduct of war, in which the energy of the executive is the bulwark of the national security, every thing would be to be apprehended from its plurality.

14 It must be confessed that these observations apply with principal weight to the first case supposed, that is to a plurality of magistrates of equal dignity and authority; a scheme the advocates for which are not likely to form a numerous sect: But they apply, though not with equal, yet with considerable weight, to the project of council, whose concurrence is made constitutionally necessary to the operations of the ostensible executive. An artful cabal in that council would be able to distract and to enervate the whole system of administration. If no such cabal should exist, the mere diversity of views and opinions would alone be sufficient to tincture the exercise of the executive authority with a spirit of habitual feebleness and dilatoriness.

15 But one of the weightiest objections to a plurality in the executive, and which lies as much against the last as the first plan, is that it tends to conceal faults, and destroy responsibility. Responsibility is of two kinds, to censure and to punishment. The first is the most important of the two; especially in an elective office. Man, in public trust, will much oftener act in such a manner to render him unworthy of being any longer trusted, than in such a manner as to make him obnoxious to legal punishment. But the multiplication of the executive adds to the difficulty of detection in either case. It often becomes impossible, amidst mutual accusations, to determine on whom the blame or the

punishment of a pernicious measure, or series of pernicious measures ought really to fall. It is shifted from one to another with so much dexterity, and under such plausible appearances, that the public opinion is left in suspense about the real author. The circumstances which may have led to any national miscarriage or misfortune are sometimes so complicated, that where there are a number of actors who may have had different degrees and kinds of agency, though we may clearly see upon the whole that there has been mismanagement, yet it may be impracticable to pronounce to whose account the evil which may have been incurred is truly chargeable.

16 "I was overruled by my council. The council were so divided in their opinions, that it was impossible to obtain any better resolution on the point." These and similar pretexts are constantly at hand, whether true or false. And who is there that will either take the trouble or incur the odium of a strict scrutiny into the secret springs of the transaction? Should there be found a citizen zealous enough to undertake the unpromising task, if there happen to be a collusion between the parties concerned, how easy is it to cloath the circumstances with so much ambiguity, as to render it uncertain what was the precise conduct of any of those parties?

17 In the single instance in which the governor of this state is coupled with a council, that is in the appointment to offices, we have seen the mischiefs of it in the view now under consideration. Scandalous appointments to important offices have been made. Some cases indeed have been so flagrant, that ALL PARTIES have agreed in the impropriety of the thing. When enquiry has been made, the blame has been laid by the governor on the members of the council; who on their part have charged it upon his nomination: While the people remain altogether at a loss to determine by whose influence their interests have been committed to hands so unqualified, and so manifestly improper. In tenderness to individuals, I forbear to descend to particulars.

18 It is evident from these considerations, that the plurality of the executive tends to deprive the people of the two greatest securities they can have for the faithful exercise of any delegated power; first, the restraints of public opinion, which lose their efficacy as well on account of the division of the censure attendant on bad measures among a number, as on account of the uncertainty on whom it ought to fall; and secondly, the opportunity of discovering with facility and clearness the misconduct of the persons they trust, in order either to their removal from office, or to their actual punishment, in cases which admit of it.

19 In England the king is a perpetual magistrate; and it is a maxim, which has obtained for the sake of the public peace, that he is unaccountable for his administration, and his person sacred. Nothing therefore can be wiser in that kingdom than to annex to the king a constitutional council, who may be responsible to the nation for the advice they give. Without this there would be no responsiblity whatever in the executive department; an idea inadmissible in a free government. But even there the king is not bound by the resolutions of his council, though they are answerable for the advice they give. He is the absolute master of his own conduct, in the exercise of his office; and may observe or disregard the council given to him at his sole discretion.

20 But in a republic, where every magistrate ought to be personally responsible for his behaviour in office, the reason which in the British constitution dictates the propriety of a council not only ceases to apply, but turns against the institution. In the monarchy of Great-Britain, it furnishes a substitute for the prohibited responsibility of the chief magistrate; which serves in some degree as a hostage to the national justice for his good behaviour. In the American republic it would serve to destroy, or would greatly diminish the intended and necessary responsibility of the chief magistrate himself.

The idea of a council to the executive, which has so generally obtained in the state constitutions, has been derived from that maxim of republican jealousy, which considers power as safer in the hands of a number of men than of a single man. If the maxim should be admitted to be applicable to the case, I should contend that the advantage on that side would not counterballance the numerous disadvantages on the opposite side. But

21   I do not think the rule at all applicable to the executive power. I clearly concur in opinion in this particular with a writer whom the celebrated Junius pronounces to be "deep, solid and ingenious," that, "the executive power is more easily confined when it is one."[1] That it is far more safe there should be a single object for the jealousy and watchfulness of the people; and in a word that all multiplication of the executive is rather dangerous than friendly to liberty.

  A little consideration will satisfy us, that the species of security sought for in the multiplication of the executive is unattainable. Numbers must be so great as to render combination difficult; or they are rather a source of danger than of security. The united credit and influence of several individuals must be more formidable to liberty than the credit and influence of either of them separately. When power therefore is placed in the hands of so small a number of men, as to admit of their interests and views being easily combined in a common enterprise, by an artful leader, it becomes more liable to abuse and more dangerous when abused, than if it be lodged in the hands of one man; who

22   from the very circumstance of his being alone will be more narrowly watched and more readily suspected, as who cannot unite so great a mass of influence as when he is associated with others. The Decemvirs of Rome, whose name denotes their number,[2] were more to be dreaded in their usurpation than any ONE of them would have been. No person would think of proposing an executive much more numerous than that body, from six to a dozen have been suggested for the number of the council. The extreme of these numbers is not too great for an easy combination; and from such a combination America would have more to fear, than from the ambition of any single individual. A council to a magistrate, who is himself responsible for what he does, are generally nothing better than a clog upon his good intentions; are often the instruments and accomplices of his bad, and are almost always a cloak to his faults.

  I forbear to dwell upon the subject of expence; though it be evident that if the council should be numerous enough to answer the principal end, aimed at by the institution, the

23   salaries of the members, who must be drawn from their homes to reside at the seat of government, would form an item in the catalogue of public expenditures, too serious to be incurred for an object of equivocal utility.

  I will only add, that prior to the appearance of the constitution, I rarely met with an

24   intelligent man from any of the states, who did not admit as the result of experience, that the UNITY of the Executive of this state was one of the best of the distinguishing features of our constitution.

[1]De Lome. (Publius)
[2]*Ten.* (Publius)

PUBLIUS.

REVIEWING THE MAIN IDEAS
1. In paragraph 13 Hamilton gives two reasons that legislatures should act slowly. State both reasons in your own words.
2. In paragraph 11 Hamilton gives two reasons that plurality in the executive would keep it from acting swiftly. State both reasons in your own words.
3. In paragraphs 15–18 Hamilton explains why plurality would also keep the executive branch from being accountable to the people. Explain Hamilton's reasoning in your own words.
4. Do you agree with Hamilton's reasoning that plurality in the executive branch would be a bad thing? Why or why not?

FEDERALIST 78

The Constitution states that once federal judges are appointed they are to hold office "during good Behaviour." This means that unless they are impeached for misbehavior and convicted, they remain in office. Some Antifederalists hated this idea. They thought that federal judges should hold office for only a certain number of years. In *Federalist* 78 Hamilton argued against their view. He gave two arguments that judges should hold office during good behavior instead of for only a certain number of years. One argument was based on the idea that judges need special legal skills and knowledge. Hamilton said that after going to all the time and trouble of gaining these skills and knowledge, nobody would want to take a job that would not last. The other argument was based on the idea that judges need to be able to make independent judgments. If a judge were appointed for only a certain number of years, then he or she would not have the independence to make his or her own decisions. The legislature could threaten the judge by saying "Unless you do as we say, we will not reappoint you."

Of these two arguments, the second was more controversial. After all, why *should* judges be independent of the legislature? Hamilton thought independence was needed so that judges could exercise judicial review, which means overruling laws that are not allowed by Constitution. But many Antifederalists thought that the legislature should decide for itself whether or not its laws were constitutional. They did not agree that judges should have the power of judicial review. Thus, in order to explain why judges should be independent, Hamilton also had to explain why they should have the power of judicial review.

The Federalist No. 78: HAMILTON

May 28, 1788

To the People of the State of New York.

1 We proceed now to an examination of the judicary department of the proposed government.

In unfolding the defects of the existing confederation, the utility and necessity of a federal judicature have been clearly pointed out. It is the less necessary to recapitulate the considerations there urged; as the propriety of the institution in the abstract is not

2 disputed: The only questions which have been raised being relative to the manner of constituting it, and to its extent. To these points therefore our observations shall be confined.

The manner of constituting it seems to embrace these several objects—1st. The mode of appointing the judges. 2d. The tenure by which they are to hold their places. 3d. The

3 partition of the judiciary authority between different courts, and their relations to each other.

First. As to the mode of appointing the judges; This is the same with that of appointing

4 the officers of the union in general, and has been so fully discussed in the last two numbers, that nothing can be said here which would not be useless repetition.

Second. As to the tenure by which the judges are to hold their places: This chiefly

5 concerns their duration in office; the provisions for their support; and the precautions for their responsibility.

According to the plan of the convention, all the judges who may be appointed by the United States are to hold their offices *during good behaviour,* which is conformable to the most approved of the state constitutions; and among the rest, to that of this state. Its propriety having been drawn into question by the adversaries of that plan, is no light symptom of the rage for objection which disorders their imaginations and judgments.

6 The standard of good behaviour for the continuance in office of the judicial magistracy is certainly one of the most valuable of the modern improvements in the practice of government. In a monarchy it is an excellent barrier to the despotism of the prince: In a republic

it is a no less excellent barrier to the encroachments and oppressions of the representative body. And it is the best expedient which can be devised in any government, to secure a steady, upright and impartial administration of the laws.

7 Whoever attentively considers the different departments of power must perceive, that in a government in which they are separated from each other, the judiciary, from the nature of its functions, will always be the least dangerous to the political rights of the constitution; because it will be least in a capacity to annoy or injure them. The executive not only dispenses the honors, but holds the sword of the community. The legislature not only commands the purse, but prescribes the rules by which the duties and rights of every citizen are to be regulated. The judiciary on the contrary has no influence over either the sword or the purse, no direction either of the strength or of the wealth of the society, and can take no active resolution whatever. It may truly be said to have neither Force nor Will, but merely judgment; and must ultimately depend upon the aid of the executive arm even for the efficacy of its judgments.

8 This simple view of the matter suggests several important consequences. It proves incontestibly that the judiciary is beyond comparison the weakest of the three departments of power,[1] that it can never attack with success either of the other two; and that all possible care is requisite to enable it to defend itself against their attacks. It equally proves, that though individual oppression may now and then proceed from the courts of justice, the general liberty of the people can never be endangered from that quarter. I mean, so long as the judiciary remains truly distinct from both the legislative and executive. For I agree that "there is no liberty, if the power of judging be not separated from the legislative and executive powers."[2] And it proves, in the last place, that as liberty can have nothing to fear from the judiciary alone, but would have every thing to fear from its union with either of the other departments; that as all the effects of such an union must ensue from a dependence of the former on the latter, notwithstanding a nominal and apparent separation; that as from the natural feebleness of the judiciary, it is in continual jeopardy of being overpowered, awed or influenced by its coordinate branches; and that as nothing can contribute so much to its firmness and independence, as permanency in office, this quality may therefore be justly regarded as an indispensable ingredient in its constitution; and in a great measure as the citadel of the public justice and the public security.

9 The complete independence of the courts is peculiarly essential in a limited constitution. By a limited constitution I understand one which contains certain specified exceptions to the legislative authority; such for instance as that it shall pass no bills of attainder, no *ex post facto* laws, and the like. Limitations of this kind can be preserved in practice no other way than through the medium of the courts of justice; whose duty it must be to declare all acts contrary to the manifest tenor of the constitution void. Without this, all the reservations of particular rights or privileges would amount to nothing.

10 Some perplexity respecting the right of the courts to pronounce legislative acts void, because contrary to the constitution, has arisen from an imagination that the doctrine would imply a superiority of the judiciary to the legislative power. It is urged that the authority which can declare the acts of another void, must necessarily be superior to the one whose acts may be declared void. As this doctrine is of great importance in all the American constitutions, a brief discussion of the grounds on which it rests cannot be unacceptable.

11 There is no position which depends on clearer principles, than that every act of a delegated authority, contrary to the tenor of the commission under which it is exercised, is void. No legislative act therefore contrary to the constitution can be valid. To deny this would be to affirm that the deputy is greater than his principal; that the servant is above his master; that the representatives of the people are superior to the people themselves;

[1] The celebrated Montesquieu speaking of them says, "of the three powers above mentioned, the JUDICIARY is next to nothing." Spirit of Laws, vol. 1, page 186. (Publius)
[2] Idem. page 181. (Publius)

that men acting by virtue of powers may do not only what their powers do not authorise, but what they forbid.

12   If it be said that the legislative body are themselves the constitutional judges of their own powers, and that the construction they put upon them is conclusive upon the other departments, it may be answered, that this cannot be the natural presumption, where it is not be collected from any particular provisions in the constitution. It is not otherwise to be supposed that the constitution could intend to enable the representatives of the people to substitute their *will* to that of their constituents. It is far more rational to suppose that the courts were designed to be an intermediate body between the people and the legislature, in order, among other things, to keep the latter within the limits assigned to their authority. The interpretation of the laws is the proper and peculiar province of the courts. A constitution is in fact, and must be, regarded by the judges as a fundamental law. It therefore belongs to them to ascertain its meaning as well as the meaning of any particular act proceeding from the legislative body. If there should happen to be an irreconcileable variance between the two, that which has the superior obligation and validity ought of course to be preferred to the statute, the intention of the people to the intention of their agents.

13   Nor does this conclusion by any means suppose a superiority of the judicial to the legislative power. It only supposes that the power of the people is superior to both; and that where the will of the legislature declared in its statutes, stands in opposition to that of the people declared in the constitution, the judges ought to be governed by the latter, rather than the former. They ought to regulate their decisions by the fundamental laws, rather than by those which are not fundamental.

14   This exercise of judicial discretion in determining between two contradictory laws, is exemplified in a familiar instance. It not uncommonly happens, that there are two statutes existing at one time, clashing in whole or in part with each other, and neither of them containing any repealing clause or expression. In such a case, it is the province of the courts to liquidate and fix their meaning and operation: So far as they can by any fair construction be reconciled to each other; reason and law conspire to dictate that this should be done. Where this is impracticable, it becomes a matter of necessity to give effect to one, in exclusion of the other. The rule which has obtained in the courts for determining their relative validity is that the last in order of time shall be preferred to the first. But this is mere rule of construction, not derived from any positive law, but from the nature and reason of the thing. It is a rule not enjoined upon the courts by legislative provision, but adopted by themselves, as consonant to truth and propriety, for the direction of their conduct as interpreters of the law. They thought it reasonable, that between the interfering acts of an *equal* authority, that which was the last indication of its will, should have the preference.

15   But in regard to the interfering acts of a superior and subordinate authority, of an original and derivative power, the nature and reason of the thing indicate the converse of that rule as proper to be followed. They teach us that the prior act of a superior ought to be preferred to the subsequent act of an inferior and subordinate authority; and that, accordingly, whenever a particular statute contravenes the constitution, it will be the duty of the judicial tribunals to adhere to the latter, and disregard the former.

16   It can be of no weight to say, that the courts on the pretence of a repugnancy, may substitute their own pleasure to the constitutional intentions of the legislature. This might as well happen in the case of two contradictory statutes; or it might as well happen in every adjudication upon any single statute. The courts must declare the sense of the law; and if they should be disposed to exercise WILL instead of JUDGMENT, the consequence would equally be the substitution of their pleasure to that of the legislative body. The observation, if it proved any thing, would prove that there ought to be no judges distinct from that body.

If then the courts of justice are to be considered as the bulwarks of a limited constitution against legislative encroachments, this consideration will afford a strong argument

17 for the permanent tenure of judicial offices, since nothing will contribute so much as this to that independent spirit in the judges, which must be essential to the faithful performance of so arduous a duty.

This independence of the judges is equally requisite to guard the constitution and the rights of individuals from the effects of those ill humours which the arts of designing men, or the influence of particular conjunctures, sometimes disseminate among the peo-

18 ple themselves, and which, though they speedily give place to better information and more deliberate reflection, have a tendency in the mean time to occasion dangerous innovations in the government, and serious oppressions of the minor party in the community. Though I trust the friends of the proposed constitution will never concur with its enemies[1] in questioning that fundamental principle of republican government, which admits the right of the people to alter or abolish the established constitution whenever they find it inconsistent with their happiness; yet it is not to be inferred from this principle, that the representatives of the people, whenever a momentary inclination happens to lay hold of a majority of their constituents incompatible with the provisions in the existing constitution, would on that account be justifiable in a violation of those provisions; or that the courts would be under a greater obligation to connive at infractions in this shape, than when they had proceeded wholly from the cabals of the representative body. Until the people have by some solemn and authoritative act annulled or changed the established form, it is binding upon themselves collectively, as well as individually; and no presumption, or even knowledge of their sentiments, can warrant their representatives in a departure from it, prior to such an act. But it is easy to see that it would require an uncommon portion of fortitude in the judges to do their duty as faithful guardians of the constitution, where legislative invasions of it had been instigated by the major voice of the community.

But it is not with a view to infractions of the constitution only that the independence of the judges may be an essential safeguard against the effects of occasional ill humours in the society. These sometimes extend no farther than to the injury of the private rights of particular classes of citizens, by unjust and partial laws. Here also the firmness of the judicial magistracy is of vast importance in mitigating the severity, and confining the operation of such laws. It not only serves to moderate the immediate mischiefs of those which may have been passed, but it operates as a check upon the legislative body in passing them; who, perceiving that obstacles to the success of an iniquitous intention are to be expected from the scruples of the courts, are in a manner compelled by the

19 very motives of the injustice they meditate, to qualify their attempts. This is a circumstance calculated to have more influence upon the character of our governments, than but few may be aware of. The benefits of the integrity and moderation of the judiciary have already been felt in more states than one; and though they may have displeased those whose sinister expectations they may have disappointed, they must have commanded the esteem and applause of all the virtuous and disinterested. Considerate men of every description ought to prize whatever will tend to beget or fortify that temper in the courts; as no man can be sure that he may not be tomorrow the victim of a spirit of injustice, by which he may be a gainer to-day. And every man must now feel that the inevitable tendency of such a spirit is to sap the foundations of public and private confidence, and to introduce in its stead, universal distrust and distress.

That inflexible and uniform adherence to the rights of the constitution and of individuals, which we perceive to be indispensable in the courts of justice, can certainly not be expected from judges who hold their offices by a temporary commission. Periodical appointments, however regulated, or by whomsoever made, would in some way or other be fatal to their necessary independence. If the power of making them was committed

[1]Vide Protest of the minority of the convention of Pennsylvania, Martin's speech, &c.
(Publius)

20 either to the executive or legislature, there would be danger of an improper complaisance to the branch which possessed it; if to both, there would an unwillingness to hazard the displeasure of either; if to the people, or to persons chosen by them for the special purpose, there would be too great a disposition to consult popularity, to justify a reliance that nothing would be consulted but the constitution and the laws.

There is yet a further and a weighty reason for the permanency of the judicial offices; which is deducible from the nature of the qualifications they require. It has been frequently remarked with great propriety, that a voluminous code of laws is one of the

21 inconveniences necessarily connected with the advantages of a free government. To avoid an arbitrary discretion in the courts, it is indispensable that they should be bound down by strict rules and precedents, which serve to define and point out their duty in every particular case that comes before them; and it will readily be conceived from the variety of controversies which grow out of the folly and wickedness of mankind, that the records of those precedents must unavoidably swell to a very considerable bulk, and must demand long and laborious study to acquire a competent knowledge of them. Hence it is that there can be but few men in the society, who will have sufficient skill in the laws to qualify them for the stations of judges. And making the proper deductions for the ordinary depravity of human nature, the number must be still smaller of those who united the requisite integrity with the requisite knowledge. These considerations apprise us, that the government can have no great option between fit characters; and that a temporary duration in office, which would naturally discourage such characters from quitting a lucrative line of practice to accept a seat on the bench, would have a tendency to throw the administration of justice into hands less able, and less well qualified to conduct it with utility and dignity. In the present circumstances of this country, and in those in which it is likely to be for a long time to come, the disadvantages on this score would be greater than they may at first sight appear; but it must be confessed that they are far inferior to those which present themselves under the other aspects of the subject.

Upon the whole there can be no room to doubt that the convention acted wisely in copying from the models of those constitutions which have established *good behaviour* as the tenure of their judicial offices in point of duration; and that so far from being

22 blameable on this account, their plan would have been inexcuseably defective if it had wanted this important feature of good government. The experience of Great Britain affords an illustrious comment on the excellence of the institution.

PUBLIUS.

REVIEWING THE MAIN IDEAS

1. In paragraph 21 Hamilton says that finding people with the special skills necessary to be good judges is even harder in a republic than in countries with others forms of government. Why?
2. Hamilton says he is not afraid that judicial review would make judges too powerful, because the judiciary is the weakest of the three branches. Study paragraph 7, and then explain the reason that Hamilton gives for considering this branch the weakest.
3. Some Antifederalists worried that if judges were given the power of judicial review, they would use this as an excuse to overrule any laws that they did not like, even if the laws were allowed by the Constitution. Study paragraph 16. What argument does Hamilton use to oppose this view?
4. Do you think that judges should be elected or appointed? Support your answer.

MAKING AN ANALYTICAL OUTLINE

One of the most useful ways to take notes is to organize your information into an outline. Outlining can also help you read with greater understanding. There are, however, many different kinds of outlines. The kind that may be best for studying one piece of writing may not be best for studying another.

Some writings, like the *Federalist Papers,* try to persuade readers to accept or reject certain opinions. The writings offer arguments, which are reasons for or against the opinions. The kind of outline that is most helpful for understanding persuasive writing is called an analytical outline. Analytical outlines break down arguments into their logical parts.

Following is a simple analytical outline of the first four paragraphs of *Federalist* 51, by James Madison. The outline is incomplete. After studying *Federalist* 51, fill in the blanks in the outline.

I. *Madison states a problem.* How can we make sure that each of the three branches of the government keeps in its proper place instead of _____

_____ ?

II. *Madison analyzes the problem.*
   A. Three different methods of keeping the branches in their proper places might be considered:
     1. Maybe something outside the government can keep them in their proper places.

     2. Maybe each branch will stay in its proper place all by itself.

     3. Maybe each branch can be made to _____ .

   B. In view of these facts, the original question ("How can we make sure that each branch of government keeps in its proper place?") turns into a simpler question: "Which method of keeping the branches in their proper places should we attempt?"

III. *Madison considers the first method.* The first method is to find something outside the government that can keep the branches in their proper places. But Madison says this will not work; in his words,

"exterior provisions" are "_____ ."

IV. *Madison considers the second method.* The second method is simply to hope that each branch will

stay in its proper place all by itself. But Madison says this will not work either, because _____

_____ .

V. *Madison reaches a conclusion.* Because the first and second methods of keeping the branches in their proper places will not work, the third method is our only hope.

VI. *Madison explains his conclusion.*
   A. Each branch must be given a way to protect itself when other branches try to intrude on its powers. Madison proposes a system of checks and balances to provide this protection.

   B. The members of each branch must also be given _____ .
   There are two ways to give them these.
     1. No branch should have much to do with selecting the members of the other branches. The reason for following this principle is to make sure that each branch has a different outlook.

     (Madison admits that the principle must be violated in the case of the _____ branch.)

     2. No branch should have much to do with _____

_____ .

     The reason for following this principle is to make sure that the branches are not

_____ .

LANDMARK CASES OF THE SUPREME COURT

- Can members of a religious group keep their children out of school?
- Can the president take over the nation's steel mills?
- Can a student be suspended from school for wearing a black armband to protest a war?
- Can high school students say whatever they like in a school newspaper?

Can you guess what these questions have in common? All four were answered by reading the Constitution! You may find this surprising. The Constitution does not say anything about religious groups and education, steel mills, armbands, or school newspapers. The Constitution does, however, say things about freedom of religion, the powers and duties of the president, and freedom of speech. The Constitution is our nation's highest authority for answering questions about the people's rights and the government's powers. These two subjects affect everyday life in hundreds of important ways.

But who decides what the Constitution means? It is not easy to decide what the authors of the Constitution meant when they wrote it, yet somebody must decide. Who?

The answer to this question has two parts. The first part is that many different groups of people decide what the Constitution means—the three branches of the federal government, and every state and local government, too. Each group must decide what the Constitution means in order to know the right way to do its work. But you can see why this part of the answer is incomplete. If many different groups decide what the Constitution means, they might disagree. Who settles their disagreements? Disagreements about the meaning of the Constitution are settled in the federal courts.

There are three levels of federal courts. Usually disagreements about the Constitution begin at the lowest level—the federal district court. If a decision made at the district level is appealed, the disagreement is carried to a federal court of appeals. An appeal is a request for a decision made in a trial court to be reviewed by a higher court. A decision made in a federal court of appeals can be appealed to a still higher authority, the United States Supreme Court.

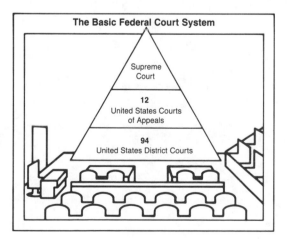

The Basic Federal Court System

Supreme
Court

12
United States Courts
of Appeals

94
United States District Courts

Because the Constitution does not explain how the Supreme Court should be organized, these details are left to Congress. Members of the Supreme Court are appointed by the president and approved by the Senate. The judges of the Supreme Court are called justices. There is one chief justice, who presides over (is in charge of) meetings. The other justices are called associate justices. Currently the Supreme Court has nine members. This number has not changed since 1869. The number of members is odd rather than even so that tie votes cannot occur. A majority vote, such as five to four or seven to two, determines the case. Sometimes ties occur anyway because one member of the Court is absent or does not participate in a case for some other reason. If a tie vote occurs, the decision of the lower court stands.

The Supreme Court does not have to hear every appeal. Members of the Court decide what they think are the most important cases. Whenever the Supreme Court accepts a case, its decision is final.

In this section of *The Constitution: Past, Present and Future* you will find 26 of the most important cases settled by the Supreme Court. They are called "landmark" cases because they are reference points for deciding what the Constitution means. You will learn about narrow definitions of the Constitution and about broad definitions of the Constitution. Cases selected by the Supreme Court are not only important but also exciting. Most of them start with stories about ordinary people, sometimes even students like you. But the cases end with decisions about the very meaning of liberty and our form of government.

1. *MARBURY V. MADISON**
5 U.S. (1 Cranch) 137 (1803)**

WHAT WAS THIS CASE ABOUT?

The story. The time was early 1801. The Federalist party had been defeated by the Democratic–Republicans in the presidential and congressional elections. However, the winners of the election were not due to take office until March 4. In the meantime the Federalists were determined to do whatever they could to hold their party's power. One action they could take was to appoint supporters of the Federalist party to offices that were not filled by election. So, they chose a number of party supporters as justices of the peace in the District of Columbia. These people were nominated by the outgoing president, John Adams, and confirmed by the Senate at the last minute—on March 3. Their "midnight appointments" seemed to be just in time. But no one could take office as a new justice of the peace until his commission had been delivered to him. The job of delivering it fell to the acting secretary of state, John Marshall. The next day when the new president, Thomas Jefferson, took over, he found that John Marshall had not had time to deliver all of the commissions before his term of office ended. Jefferson was delighted. He immediately ordered his new secretary of state, James Madison, not to deliver the rest of the commissions. The people who had been confirmed by the Senate as justices of the peace could not take office after all!

William Marbury, one of the people whose commission was not delivered, sued James Madison. Marbury took advantage of a law passed by Congress that allowed him to make this kind of complaint directly to the Supreme Court. He asked the Court to order Madison to deliver the commission even though this request meant disobeying the president. Probably he expected the Court to do as he asked because John Marshall had been appointed chief justice of the Supreme Court. You remember that until James Madison took over as secretary of state on March 4, Marshall had held that job. Marshall was a strong Federalist. Moreover, he might have felt a personal responsibility to Marbury because he had not been able to deliver Marbury's commission in time.

The question. As Chief Justice Marshall saw it, the question before the Court had three parts. First, did Marbury have a right to receive the commission? Second, if he did have a right to the commission, was the government now required to make amends? Finally, if the government was required to make amends, would it have to order Madison to deliver Marbury's commission, as Marbury requested?

The issues. One might have thought that Chief Justice Marshall would want Marbury to receive his commission. Perhaps he did, but he cared even more about something else—the power of the Supreme Court itself. He considered it deeply important that the Court have a role in the system of checks and balances. Specifically, he wanted the Court to be able to decide if laws passed by Congress were constitutional. Whether or not the Court had this power of **judicial review** had not yet been decided. Marshall posed the question before the Court in the way he did in order to discuss judicial review.

HOW WAS THE CASE DECIDED?

Two years later, in an opinion written by the chief justice himself, the Court ruled against ordering James Madison to deliver Marbury's commission. Is this ruling what you expected?

WHAT DID THE COURT SAY ABOUT GOVERNMENTAL POWERS?

First let's see how the Court reached its decision. Remember that Marshall had said that the question before it had three parts. Each part had to be answered before the Court could go on to the next part. So, the Court's reasoning went through three steps.

Step 1. Did Marbury have a right to the commission? Pointing to a law passed by

---

*The name of a court case is usually italicized. The two names represent the people involved in each case. The "*v.*" stands for "versus," which means "against."
**These numbers are the case citation. "5 U.S." means that the case can be found in Volume 5 of the *United States Reports*. "(1 Cranch)" means that this corresponds to Volume 1 of an earlier set of case reports, now discontinued, kept by a man named Cranch. "137" is the number of the page on which the case begins. "1803" designates the year in which the case was decided.

Congress, which told how justices of the peace should be appointed for the District of Columbia, the Court said that he did.

Step 2. Was the government required to make amends? The Court said that when government officials (such as Madison) hurt people (such as Marbury) by neglecting legal duties (such as delivering commissions), our laws require that a remedy be found for the injury.

Step 3. If the government was required to make amends, did that mean that Madison must be ordered to deliver Marbury's commission as Marbury had requested?

Marbury had asked that the Supreme Court simply order Madison to deliver the commission. Here Chief Justice Marshall did something surprising. Instead of giving a simple yes or no answer, he said yes, a court could issue such an order, but no, this was not the right court to issue it.

Why wasn't this the right court to issue it? Remember that Marbury had taken advantage of a law passed by Congress that allowed complaints such as his to be taken straight to the Supreme Court instead of going through lower courts. However, Chief Justice Marshall said that this law was unconstitutional. You know that the Constitution mentions several kinds of cases that can be brought straight to the Supreme Court. All other kinds of cases must go through lower courts first. Marbury's lawsuit, said the chief justice, was one of the kinds of cases that must go through lower courts first. It did not matter that Congress had passed a law saying something different, he said, because the Constitution is a higher law. When two laws come into conflict, judges must obey the higher of them. Besides, judges take an oath to support the Constitution.

Do you see how cleverly Marshall wrote the Court's opinion? Sometimes, in a game of chess, a player gives up something in order to get something even better. The player allows a piece to be captured because it is the only way to get the other pieces into a stronger position. This example is something like what Marshall did. He gave up the power, granted to the Court by Congress, of hearing lawsuits such as Marbury's before lower courts had heard them. But the way that he gave up this power was to claim for the Court an even greater power. This greater power was the power of judicial review itself: the power to decide if laws made by Congress are allowed by the Constitution.

WHAT IMPLICATIONS DID THIS CASE HAVE FOR THE FUTURE?

Until 1803 nobody knew if judges really would be able to exercise such a power. In other words, nobody knew if the judicial branch would be able to play a role in the system of checks and balances at all. Without judicial review, Congress would decide for itself on the constitutionality of the laws it passed. By writing the opinion of the Court in *Marbury v. Madison,* Chief Justice Marshall changed all that forever. Today the judicial branch has taken its place as an equal to the legislative and executive branches. By deciding on the constitutionality of the actions of the other two branches, it is the nation's final authority on the meaning of the Constitution itself.

BRAIN TEASERS

1. What kinds of cases does the Constitution state may be heard by the Supreme Court?
2. If Chief Justice Marshall had not been eager to speak out on the subject of judicial review, how might his opinion have differed from the one he wrote?
3. If the judicial branch had not acquired the power of judicial review, then Congress would be its own judge of the constitutionality of its laws. Do you think it would be good or bad for Congress to have this power? Why?

2. *MARTIN V. HUNTER'S LESSEE*
14 U.S. (1 Wheat) 304 (1816)

WHAT WAS THIS CASE ABOUT?

The story. This case arose from an argument over who owned a certain piece of property in Virginia. Originally, the land had been owned by an Englishman named Lord Fairfax. In 1777, during the Revolutionary War, the

Virginia legislature had passed a law saying that the land of people who were still loyal to England no longer belonged to them. One of the people affected by this law was Lord Fairfax. When Lord Fairfax died in England in 1781, the land was passed down to his American relative, Thomas Martin. But the government of Virginia gave Fairfax's land to a man named David Hunter.

Thomas Martin still considered himself to be the true owner of the land. He did not think the Virginia law was valid. Hunter disagreed. He was so sure that he, not Martin, was the true owner of the land that he even rented it to someone else. Naturally, the renter (called the "lessee") tried to have Martin **evicted**. This dispute led to a long struggle in the state courts. Finally, Virginia's highest court ruled that Hunter's lessee was right. The land's true owner, it said, was Hunter, not Martin.

Martin **appealed** his case to the United States Supreme Court. He reminded the Court of the treaties made between America and England in 1783 and 1794. These treaties promised that America would protect the rights of British subjects who had owned property in America before the Revolutionary War. Because of these treaties, he said, Virginia's 1777 law was not valid. Thus, he was the true owner after all. The Supreme Court agreed. It sent the case back to the Virginia court with orders to change its decision.

But the Virginia court refused to obey these orders. Led by Judge Spencer Roane, it denied that the Supreme Court had the authority to tell a state court what to do. So, Martin had to ask the Supreme Court for help a second time. Because the Virginia court would not obey the orders to reverse its judgment, Martin wanted the Supreme Court to reverse the Virginia court's judgment.

The question. The question before the Court was not who was the true owner of the land. That question had been asked and answered the first time Martin had appealed to the Court. This time the question was different: In cases that involve the federal Constitution, laws, and treaties, does the Constitution give federal courts the power to reverse state court judgments?

The issues. You might think that the question before the Court had already been settled in *Marbury v. Madison* (1803). After all, that case gave the Supreme Court the power of judicial review. It did not, however, settle the broader issue of just how far the power of judicial review extends. In *Marbury v. Madison,* the Supreme Court had overruled one of the other branches of the federal government. What Martin asked the Supreme Court to do in this case was overrule one of the branches of a state government.

HOW WAS THE CASE DECIDED?

Finally, in 1816, in an opinion written by Justice Joseph Story, the Supreme Court did what Martin asked. It reversed the judgment of the Virginia court.

WHAT DID THE COURT SAY ABOUT GOVERNMENTAL POWERS?

Justice Story thought that the Constitution gave the Supreme Court the power to reverse state court judgments in cases involving the federal Constitution, laws, and treaties. But how did he show that his view was correct? He might have simply quoted Article III, which says that "the judicial Power [of the United States] shall extend to all Cases . . . arising under this Constitution, the Laws of the United States, and Treaties made . . . under their Authority." But Justice Story did not stop there.

First he tried to show why various objections to his view were mistaken. One objection was that the Constitution does not affect the state governments, but only the people in them. Justice Story pointed out that the Constitution is "crowded" with provisions that affect the state governments. Another objection was that if federal judges had the power of final decision about the meaning of the federal Constitution, laws, and treaties, they might abuse it. Justice Story explained that the power of final decision has to be put somewhere.

Finally, Justice Story explained the need for uniformity. If federal judges were not allowed to reverse state court judgments, then state courts in each of the different states might interpret the federal Constitution, laws, and treaties in different ways. "The public mischiefs that would attend such a state of things," he said, "would be truly deplorable [bad; disgraceful]."

WHAT IMPLICATIONS DID THIS CASE HAVE FOR THE FUTURE?

This case helps us understand some of the stresses and strains on our system of government. Under our Constitution, power is divided into two levels, state and national. This system of government is called **federalism**. State governments are not merely regional offices of the national government; they are truly independent. The founders of our country thought that federalism would help to preserve liberty. However, this safeguard of liberty has a price—a greater chance of conflict. Our history is full of various kinds of conflicts between the states and the national government.

Usually, as in *Martin v. Hunter's Lessee,* the national government has won these conflicts. Thus, there has been a slow drift of power from the states to the national government. However, the drift of power has often been challenged and will no doubt continue to be challenged.

Notice, though, that Justice Story did not claim that federal courts could overrule state courts in all cases. He said only that they could overrule state courts in cases involving the United States Constitution, laws, and treaties. In matters that did not involve the federal Constitution, laws, and treaties, the judgments of state courts would be final. This principle still holds.

BRAIN TEASERS

1. As you have just read, federal courts can reverse state court judgments only in cases involving the federal Constitution, laws, and treaties. How did *Martin v. Hunter's Lessee* involve federal laws or treaties?
2. Justice Story said that if state courts in each of the different states were allowed to interpret the federal Constitution, laws, and treaties in different ways, "the public mischiefs that would attend such a state of things would be truly deplorable." What kinds of "public mischiefs" do you think he had in mind? Why would they be "deplorable?"
3. Find the article and paragraph of the Constitution that says that the Constitution

and the laws and treaties made to help carry it out "shall be the Supreme Law of the Land." What does this provision say about state governments?

3. McCULLOCH V. MARYLAND
17 U.S. (4 Wheat) 304 (1819)

WHAT WAS THIS CASE ABOUT?

The story. In 1791 Congress passed a law that set up a Bank of the United States. The bank helped American manufacturing by making loans to businesses. Congress, however, had granted the bank only a 20-year **charter.** Over these two decades, the bank became unpopular. An attempt to renew its charter in 1811 failed, and it went out of business. A number of states took advantage of this situation and began chartering banks of their own.

After the War of 1812, the federal government needed money to pay for the war. But instead of being able to borrow money from one central bank, it had to deal with many state banks. Thus, Congress set up a Second Bank of the United States in 1816. The states opposed the new national bank because their own banks were losing business to it. Several states struck back. They passed laws that hindered the national bank in various ways. For instance, they placed heavy taxes on branches of the national bank within their borders. The bank refused to pay these taxes.

One of the states that tried to tax the national bank was Maryland. When the Maryland branch of the national bank refused to pay the taxes, the state government sued the bank's cashier, James McCulloch. A year later, in 1819, the legal battle between McCulloch and Maryland reached the Supreme Court.

The question. As seen by John Marshall, the chief justice, the question before the Court had two parts. First, does the Constitution give Congress the power to establish a national bank? If so, then does the Constitution allow Maryland to tax that bank?

The issues. The question of whether or not the Constitution gives Congress the power to establish a bank had come up once before. In

1791, after Congress had passed the bill setting up the First Bank of the United States, President Washington had asked his cabinet for advice. He saw that although Article I, Section 8, of the Constitution lists the powers of Congress, it does not include the power to charter a bank. On the other hand, it states that besides the listed powers, Congress may also make all laws that are "necessary and proper" for carrying out the listed powers.

Thomas Jefferson, the secretary of state, and Alexander Hamilton, the secretary of the treasury, presented Washington with sharply opposing views. Hamilton considered the power to charter a bank constitutional because it had "a natural relation" to the powers of collecting taxes and regulating trade, listed in Section 8. By contrast, Jefferson said that while the power to charter a bank may be "convenient" for carrying out this power, it was not "necessary" to it. Therefore, he said that the power to charter a bank was unconstitutional.

Finding Hamilton's argument more convincing, Washington signed the bank bill into law. Now, though—a full generation later—the issue was reopened over the Second Bank of the United States. Maryland wanted the Supreme Court to interpret the Constitution in the way that Washington had rejected 28 years previously.

HOW WAS THE CASE DECIDED?

Led by Chief Justice Marshall, the Court ruled that the Constitution allowed Congress to establish a national bank but that it did not allow Maryland to tax the bank.

WHAT DID THE COURT SAY ABOUT GOVERNMENTAL POWERS?

Remember that Jefferson's argument against the First Bank of the United States had rested on a narrow interpretation of the word "necessary" in the "necessary and proper" clause. The state of Maryland used the same argument against the Second Bank of the United States. Chief Justice Marshall, however, said that Maryland's interpretation of the Constitution was not broad enough. In ordinary speech, he explained, when we say that certain means are "necessary" to an end we don't usually mean that we can't achieve the end without them. Rather we mean merely that they are "calculated to produce" the end. Certainly, the power to charter a bank is calculated to help carry out the other constitutional powers, so the Constitution permits it.

The second question before the Court was whether or not the Constitution allows Maryland to tax the national bank. Marshall said that if the states could tax one of the federal government's activities, they could tax any of them. But "the power to tax," said Marshall, "involves the power to destroy." He meant that by taxation, the states could prevent the federal government from accomplishing any of its purposes. This could not be permitted because of the wording in the second paragraph of Article VI. According to this "supremacy clause," the Constitution and laws of the federal government come before the constitutions and laws of the states.

WHAT IMPLICATIONS DID THIS CASE HAVE FOR THE FUTURE?

As new cases arise, members of the Supreme Court try to settle them by using principles that have been developed in earlier cases. What principles does this case involve?

• The principle of implied powers

Some powers given the federal government by the Constitution are listed. These are called **enumerated powers.** Others, however, are understood as given because they are needed to help carry out the enumerated powers. These powers are called **implied powers.** The principle of implied powers greatly enlarged our understanding of what the Constitution allows the federal government to do.

• The principle of national supremacy

The federal Constitution and federal laws come before the constitutions and laws of the states. This principle is easy to misunderstand. It does not mean that the federal government may make the states do whatever it pleases. The federal government has only those powers that are enumerated and implied in the Constitution. All other powers are denied to it. But when the federal government is using powers that do belong to it, the states must give way.

1. Where in the Constitution can you find the principle of implied powers? the principle of national supremacy?
2. The 10th Amendment states that "the powers not delegated to the United States by the Constitution, nor prohibited by it to the States, are reserved to the States respectively, or to the people." Early in the nation's history, many Americans thought this amendment meant that the federal government had only those powers that were actually listed in Article I, Section 8. What does John Marshall's reasoning suggest about this view?
3. Do you agree with Jefferson's "narrow" interpretation of the Constitution or with Hamilton's "broad" interpretation of the Constitution? Why?

4. *DRED SCOTT V. SANDFORD*
60 U.S. (19 How.) 393 (1857)

WHAT WAS THIS CASE ABOUT?

The story. In the mid-1800s the heated issue of slavery in the territories was on everyone's mind. One question that arose from this issue was what would happen to the status of a slave who was taken into free territory. This was the situation in which Dred Scott found himself.

In 1833 Dred Scott was purchased by an army doctor named John Emerson. As the army transferred Emerson from post to post, Scott went with him. First they went to Illinois; later they moved to the Wisconsin Territory. When Emerson was transferred yet again, he sent Scott to Missouri, a slave state, to live with his wife, Mrs. Irene Sanford Emerson. She inherited Scott when her husband died in 1843.

The key point to remember is that at this time, slavery was illegal in two of the places in which Dred Scott had lived. It was illegal in Illinois because of state law and in Wisconsin Territory because of the Missouri Compromise of 1820. Scott believed that because he had lived for five years on free soil, he should be free.

Scott's first attempt to gain his freedom came in 1846. Mrs. Emerson moved to New York and left Scott temporarily with the two sons of Scott's original owner. One son, a lawyer, was opposed to the extension of slavery. He helped Scott file a lawsuit asking the courts of the state of Missouri to declare Scott free.

In 1852, after six long years, the Supreme Court of Missouri ruled against Scott. This might have ended the story, but it did not. One year earlier, Mrs. Emerson had sent Scott to one of her brothers in New York, named John Sanford*. Meanwhile, the United States had won the war with Mexico, and its boundaries now stretched clear to California. The issue of slavery in the territories had to be settled. In 1854 Scott's original lawsuit was revived by lawyers who wanted to see the issue resolved. The feeling of the public was that a decision had to be made by the United States Supreme Court. Mrs. Emerson transferred her title of ownership of Scott to John Sanford, and Scott's case got on the **docket** of the Federal Circuit Court of Missouri. By 1857 Scott's case had finally worked its way to the Supreme Court.

The question. Roger B. Taney, the chief justice, saw the case as asking two questions. First, does the Constitution give an African American the right to start a suit in a federal court? Second, does the Constitution allow Congress to make a law that takes slaves away from people who bring them into a free territory?

The issues. If African Americans are citizens of the United States, then they must have all of the rights of other citizens, including the right to bring suit in federal court. Therefore, the first question before the court involved what the Constitution says about who is a citizen.

If slaves are property, then when Congress wants to make a law dealing with slavery, it must be limited in all of the same ways as when it wants to make a law dealing with property. Therefore, the second question before the Court involved the issue of what kinds of limits the Constitution puts on laws about property.

*You may have noticed that the Supreme Court's title of the case spelled the name Sandford with the letter "d" in the middle. The misspelling was an error made by the Supreme Court.

HOW WAS THE CASE DECIDED?

The Court ruled that the Constitution denied blacks the right to sue in federal court and denied Congress the power to make a law taking slaves away from people who bring them into a free territory.

WHAT DID THE COURT SAY ABOUT CONSTITUTIONAL RIGHTS?

One theme of the Court's opinion was the relation between race and citizenship. What Chief Justice Taney said reflected the prejudices of the day. He said that African Americans had "none of the rights and privileges" of citizens. This statement was especially startling because it applied not only to slaves, but also to free blacks.

The chief justice ignored an important fact. Whether or not free blacks were United States citizens, many states considered them state citizens. Article III, Section 2 of the Constitution says that the federal courts have jurisdiction over a number of various kinds of suits involving state citizens. Dred Scott's suit involved actions between citizens of different states. At least, then, the chief justice might have reasoned that free blacks in states that considered them state citizens could bring certain kinds of suits in federal courts.

The other theme of Chief Justice Taney's opinion concerned slavery rather than race. The Fifth Amendment contains a clause stating that nobody may be "deprived of life, liberty, or property, without due process of law." First, the chief justice reasoned that because slaves are "property," slaves cannot be taken away without "due process of law." Second, he reasoned that a law taking away the property of law-abiding citizens just because they have entered a free territory cheats them of their "due process of law." Taney's conclusion was that the Missouri Compromise of 1820 was unconstitutional. Congress should not have made a law that took slaves away from people who brought them into a free territory.

WHAT IMPLICATIONS DID THIS CASE HAVE FOR THE FUTURE?

By the time the Court made its decision, the Missouri Compromise's ban on slavery in certain federal territories had already been canceled by the Kansas–Nebraska Act of 1854. Therefore, it might seem that the Court's judgment that the Missouri Compromise was unconstitutional did not matter. But the Kansas–Nebraska Act was unpopular with people who opposed the extension of slavery. They would have liked to have seen a return to something like the Missouri Compromise. After the Court declared the Missouri Compromise unconstitutional, however, such a return was impossible. Rather than settling the controversy over slavery in the territories, *Dred Scott v. Sandford* heated it up. The Supreme Court's ruling hastened the coming of the Civil War.

One of the results of the Civil War was that the slaves were freed. Because of *Dred Scott v. Sandford,* though, merely freeing them was not enough to guarantee their citizenship. Not until 1868, when the 14th Amendment was passed, was the citizenship of African Americans guaranteed by the Constitution. As the amendment's very first sentence declares, "All persons born or naturalized in the United States, and subject to the jurisdiction thereof, are citizens of the United States and of the State wherein they reside." The 14th Amendment and other post-Civil War amendments were milestones on the road to full equality for people of all races.

BRAIN TEASERS

1. According to the Constitution, over what other kinds of suits involving state citizens do the federal courts have jurisdiction?
2. How did Article III of the Constitution contradict Chief Justice Taney's conclusion that African Americans, whether slave or free, could not bring suits in federal courts?
3. Carefully read the 13th, 14th, and 15th Amendments. How did the amendments reverse the Court's positions in *Dred Scott* on race, citizenship, and slavery?

5. *LOCHNER V. NEW YORK*
198 U.S. 45 (1905)

WHAT WAS THIS CASE ABOUT?

The story. In 1897 the legislature of the state of New York passed a law that regulated working conditions. One part of the law said that no employee in a bakery could be required, or allowed, to work more than 60 hours in one week. Why was such a law needed? The legislature thought that bakery workers and employers were not on an equal footing. Bosses could make workers agree to work long hours because the workers were afraid of losing their jobs. Even if workers wanted to work such long hours, the legislature thought that they should not be allowed to do so. Bakery work is very hard and very hot, and working long hours would hurt the workers' health. Some people also thought that laws limiting the hours of labor would make workers' family lives better. They reasoned that with shorter hours of labor, workers could spend more time with their families.

Some bakery owners were convicted of violating the law. One bakery owner named Lochner appealed his conviction. He said that the law was unconstitutional because it took away his liberty to make a contract about hours of labor with his employees. Lochner said that liberty of contract is promised by a clause in the 14th Amendment. The clause says that no state may "deprive any person of life, liberty, or property, without due process of law." From *Dred Scott v. Sandford* you remember that nearly identical wording is found in the Fifth Amendment. The difference is that in the Fifth Amendment, the wording applies to federal laws, while in the 14th Amendment, it applies to state laws. In 1905 *Lochner v. New York* reached the Supreme Court.

The question. Is it a violation of the 14th Amendment for a state to limit the number of hours that employees may be required or permitted to work?

The issues. As the Court explained, state governments have a general power to make regulations that support the safety, health, morals, and general welfare of their citizens. This power is called the "police power" because one of the meanings of the word *police* is "regulation." (*Police* need not always refer to law-enforcement officers.) New York's 1897 law about work in bakeries is a good example of the use of the police power. As you saw earlier, the law was intended to protect workers' health by limiting the time they could spend at hard, hot labor. Many people

also saw it as protecting morals by allowing workers to spend more time at home with their families. We know that the Constitution puts limits on various powers of the federal government. The basic issue of this case, however, is how the Constitution might limit the police power of the state governments.

Where in the Constitution would one look to find such limits? Several limits on the states are contained in various amendments, but the most general limit is the "due process" clause of the 14th Amendment. Read the wording of the clause again very carefully:

> "No State shall . . . deprive any person of life, liberty, or property, without due process of law. . . ."

In order to apply this clause to the New York bakery law, the Supreme Court had to make two judgments. One was deciding which freedoms are meant by the word *liberty*. Does the meaning include liberty of contract or not? The other was deciding just what is promised by the guarantee of "due process of law." Does this phrase merely limit how laws may be made and enforced, or does it also limit what they say?

How do you think the bakery owner, Lochner, wanted the Court to make these two decisions?

HOW WAS THE CASE DECIDED?

In an opinion written by Justice Rufus Wheeler Peckham, the Court ruled that the New York law limiting the hours of labor in bakeries was unconstitutional.

WHAT DID THE COURT SAY ABOUT GOVERNMENTAL POWERS?

"This court," said Justice Peckham, "has recognized the existence and upheld the exercise of the police power in many cases." He argued, however, that the New York legislature had gone too far. The problem with the New York law was that its interference with liberty of contract was improper.

Justice Peckham did not mean that the Constitution forbids all interference with liberty of contract, no matter how slight, no matter how good the reasons for it. In fact, he stressed that the Court had approved a Utah law that was somewhat similar to the New York law. The Utah law said that nobody in an underground mine could work more than eight hours a day "except in cases of emergency, where life or property is in imminent danger." Such uses of the police power, he said, were "fair, reasonable, and appropriate." They regulate liberty without taking it away. By contrast, New York's interference with liberty of contract was "unreasonable, unnecessary, and arbitrary [not decided by reason or principle]." He argued that New York's law had nothing to do with safety, morals, or general welfare, and he said that the law was not really necessary to protect health.

WHAT IMPLICATIONS DID THIS CASE HAVE FOR THE FUTURE?

As new cases come up the members of the Supreme Court try to settle them by using the same principles that they have developed in earlier cases. What principles did this case test?

- To what extent does the word *liberty* in the 14th Amendment apply to liberty of contract?
- Does the 14th Amendment's promise of "due process of law" limit not only how laws are made and enforced but also what they say? If they interfere with liberty—in this case, liberty of contract—the interference must be "fair, reasonable, and appropriate." How might this interference be judged?

Even though the Court tries to use the same principles over and over, sometimes its members change their minds about controversial issues. An opinion expressed by only one justice today might become the opinion of the majority 10, 20, or 30 years later.

Four justices **dissented,** or disagreed with the ruling. The most interesting dissenting opinion was written by Justice Oliver Wendell Holmes. "This case," he said, "is decided upon an economic theory which a large part of the country does not entertain," the theory of **laissez-faire.** According to this theory a person has "liberty to do what he likes so long as he does not interfere with the liberty of others to do the same." (The opposite theory is called **paternalism,** which says that at least in some cases, people may be kept from hurting themselves.) He went on to say that

he thought that the decision was for the citizens and their legislators, not for judges. His only duty as a judge was to see if the theory was in the Constitution, and "a Constitution is not intended to embody a particular economic theory, whether of paternalism . . . or of laissez-faire." He said that the members of the Court were acting as though the word *liberty* meant whatever opinions the justices happened to hold themselves.

Thousands of people agreed with Justice Holmes. State legislatures had begun to make more and more regulations to protect workers. They were angry that the Court had called such a law "unreasonable, unnecessary, and arbitrary."

Over the years the membership of the Supreme Court changed. Some of the new members had views different from those held by the Court in 1905; others held the same views but later changed their minds. In the 1940s the Court began to reverse all of the **precedents** it had set in cases like *Lochner v. New York.* By the 1960s this process of reversal was complete. As Justice Hugo Black said in a 1963 case called *Ferguson v. Skrupa,*

> "The doctrine that prevailed in *Lochner . . .* that due process authorizes courts to hold laws unconstitutional when they believe the legislature has acted unwisely—has long since been discarded. We have returned to the original constitutional proposition that courts do not substitute their social and economic beliefs for the judgment of legislative bodies, who are elected to pass laws."

BRAIN TEASERS

1. In your own words, write a definition of the words *laissez-faire* and *paternalism.* How did the opinion of the Court reflect laissez-faire? How did the opinion of the New York legislature reflect paternalism?
2. Justice Holmes said that choosing between laissez-faire and paternalism was a decision for the public and its legislators, not the decision of judges. You are a member of the public. Do you approve of the New York bakery law? Explain your answer.

3. What part of the Constitution was used in *Dred Scott v. Sandford* and in *Lochner v. New York?* What does this part of the Constitution state?

6. *SCHENCK V. UNITED STATES*
249 U.S. 47 (1919)

WHAT WAS THIS CASE ABOUT?

The story. In the early years of the twentieth century, most people did not want to hear the government criticized. There were several reasons for this attitude. One reason was a fear of political **radicalism.** This fear had many causes, but it was inflamed by the assassination of President McKinley in 1901. Another reason was fear of enemy sympathizers, which began with America's entry into World War I. In 1917 Congress passed a law called the Espionage Act. Among other things, the law said that during wartime obstructing the draft and trying to make soldiers disloyal or disobedient were crimes. Almost 2,000 people were accused of violating this law and were put on trial.

Charles Schenck was against the war, and he decided to do something about it. He mailed pamphlets to men who had been drafted into the armed forces. These pamphlets said that the government had no right to send American citizens to other countries to kill people. They said that to be drafted was to be enslaved and that slavery had been abolished by the 13th Amendment. They also said that the war was a plot by rich people on Wall Street. Finally, they urged soldiers not to give in to the government's bullying.

The government responded by accusing Schenck of violating the Espionage Act. It said that Schenck's pamphlets were intended to weaken the loyalty of soldiers and to obstruct military recruiting. Schenck answered the charge by saying that the Espionage Act was unconstitutional. He said that it broke the First Amendment's promise that "Congress shall make no law . . . abridging the freedom of speech." After working its way through the federal courts, the case was judged by the Supreme Court in 1919.

The question. Is it a violation of the First Amendment for Congress to make a law that would punish a person for saying to soldiers, during wartime, things such as Schenck said?

The issues. Just what is "freedom of speech"? Does this phrase mean permission to use words in any way at all—liberty to say anything to anyone, at any time, in any place, and in any way? For instance, could a reporter write false statements about a person just because the reporter did not like that person? Nobody believes that this use of speech is what the writers of the First Amendment meant when they promised freedom of speech. But does the First Amendment allow Congress to limit free speech in any way it pleases? If the First Amendment did allow this, political criticism, debate, and discussion would be impossible. The writers of the amendment wanted to liberate political speech, not to muzzle it. In *Schenck v. United States,* the Supreme Court had to decide what kinds of limits on speech should be allowed without destroying what we mean by the word *freedom.*

HOW WAS THE CASE DECIDED?

In a court opinion written by Justice Oliver Wendell Holmes, the Supreme Court **unanimously** upheld (supported) Schenck's conviction, saying that it did not violate his First Amendment right to free speech.

WHAT DID THE COURT SAY ABOUT CONSTITUTIONAL RIGHTS?

Justice Holmes admitted that "in many places and in ordinary times" Schenck would have had a right to say everything that he said in his pamphlets. However, he said that how far a person's freedom of speech extends depends on the circumstances. "The most stringent protection of free speech," he said, "would not protect a man in falsely shouting fire in a theatre and causing a panic." Justice Holmes compared that circumstance to living in a nation at war. "When a nation is at war," he said, "many things that might be said in time of peace are such a hindrance to its effort that their utterance will not be endured so long as men fight and that no Court could regard them as protected by any constitutional right." During war, he thought, the government certainly has the power to prevent obstructions to recruitment. Therefore, it also has the power to punish someone who uses words that are proven to cause such obstructions. "The question in every case," said Holmes, "is whether the words are used in such circumstances and are of such a nature as to create a clear and present danger that they will bring about the substantive evils that Congress has a right to prevent."

WHAT IMPLICATIONS DID THIS CASE HAVE FOR THE FUTURE?

Look again at the last sentence of the last paragraph. Justice Holmes expresses what is called the "clear and present danger test." This test has been used in many other cases. A famous lower court judge named Learned Hand once said that whenever the government claims that someone's speech poses a danger, judges must consider both the seriousness of the danger and the likelihood of it actually happening. For instance, suppose someone makes a speech calling the government a dictatorship and hinting that revolution would be a good idea. Overthrow is the most serious evil that can happen to the government. But that person may not be punished for his words unless they really do make this danger likely.

A number of judges have disapproved of the clear and present danger test. Remember, sometimes dissenters succeed in persuading other members of the Court to change their minds. Judge Hand himself once wrote that he was not "wholly in love" with the test. His complaint was that it made the decision about when speech may be limited "a matter of degree." He meant that it was unfortunate that this particular aspect was open to changing interpretation. Each case could result in a contradictory decision!

The most well-known opponent of the clear and present danger test was the late Justice Hugo Black. He objected to the very idea that the First Amendment's promises of freedom could be "balanced" against other governmental goals (such as wanting to prevent obstructions to recruiting soldiers). He thought that this **balancing view of free speech** destroyed freedom. Instead he proposed another approach to the First Amendment, called the **absolutist view of free speech.** People who support this view believe that the promise of freedom means that speakers may never be punished for what they say. They may, however, be punished for the place, time, or way in which they say it. A reporter could not be punished for telling a friend false statements about another person, but the reporter could be punished for writing the false statements in a newspaper article.

BRAIN TEASERS

1. Explain the balancing view of the First Amendment and the absolutist view of the First Amendment in your own words.
2. If the Supreme Court had taken an absolutist view of the First Amendment, could it still have upheld Schenck's conviction? Explain your answer.
3. Choose between the balancing view and the absolutist view of the First Amendment. Use your imagination to defend the view you choose against the criticisms that would be made by those who choose the other view.

---

7. *EVERSON V. BOARD OF EDUCATION* and *AGUILAR V. FELTON*
330 U.S. 1 (1947) and 473 U.S. 402 (1985)

WHAT WERE THESE CASES ABOUT?

The stories. Both of these cases concern government, religion, and public schools. The cases are discussed together because they show the extreme difficulty the Supreme Court has had in making consistent decisions in matters of church and state. The two stories have similar beginnings. As you will see in the next section, however, they have very different middles and ends.

The first case, *Everson v. Board of Education,* was about a school district in Ewing, New Jersey, that did not have any school buses. Children rode back and forth to school on regular city buses. The school board decided to reimburse, or pay back, parents for the money their children spent on bus fares. Because taxes were paid by all parents, all parents were reimbursed (parents who sent their children to public schools as well as parents who sent their children to religious schools). A taxpayer sued the school board and asked the courts to order that parents who sent their children to religious schools no longer be reimbursed.

The second case, *Aguilar v. Felton,* was about New York City's use of a federal grant that provided money to assist poor, educationally deprived children. The city used part of the money to pay city teachers to give remedial education to children who attended religious schools. To make sure that government did not get too involved with religion, the city also assigned supervisors to drop in on the remedial teachers unannounced. The supervisors were supposed to make sure that the remedial teaching activities did not involve religion. A taxpayer sued the city and asked the courts to order this use of the federal grant money stopped.

The questions. In both cases the taxpayers who sued said that the policies they opposed violated the "establishment clause" of the First Amendment. Therefore, the questions in the two cases were almost identical. *Everson* asked if it was a violation of the establishment clause to reimburse not only public school parents but also parents of religious-school students for bus fares spent by their children to and from school. *Aguilar* asked if it was a violation of the establishment clause to pay the salaries of public employees who taught in religious-school classrooms.

The issues. The establishment clause reads, "Congress shall make no law . . . respecting an establishment of religion." *Respecting* means "about." *Establishment of religion* means, literally, "official church." Narrowly viewed, then, the establishment clause means "Congress may make no law . . . about an official church." However, some people believe that the establishment clause was intended to ban more than an official church. They believe that it was intended to ban any contact between government and religion at all, no matter how slight. Broadly viewed, it might even mean that the slogan "In God We Trust" should be removed from coins and that Congress should stop opening its sessions with prayer.

What these two cases required the Court to do was decide if the true meaning of the establishment clause was the narrow meaning, the broad meaning, or something else in between.

You may wonder how the First Amendment can come into play in these two cases at all. After all, the First Amendment mentions only

Congress, not state or local governments. However, it was extended to state and local governments by the 14th Amendment.

HOW WERE THE CASES DECIDED?

The results of these two cases sharply differed. In *Everson* the Supreme Court ruled that the school authorities had not violated the establishment clause. In *Aguilar* it ruled that they had.

WHAT DID THE COURT SAY ABOUT CONSTITUTIONAL RIGHTS?

The opinion in *Everson* was written by Justice Hugo Black. He accepted Thomas Jefferson's view that the establishment clause builds a "wall of separation between church and state." However, he did not think that the reimbursement plan broke down that wall. In his view the plan was simply a way to further the government's interest in the education of all children. Justice Black suggested that refusing to allow reimbursement of bus fares for religious-school students was like refusing to allow policemen to protect religious-school students from traffic, refusing to allow firemen to put out a fire at a religious school, or refusing to allow religious schools the use of public highways and sidewalks. If the state provides such services at all, they are due to all citizens equally.

Later, in a 1970 case,* the Court admitted that its language about a "wall of separation" was misleading. "The line of separation," it said, "far from being a 'wall,' is a blurred, indistinct, and variable barrier depending on all the circumstances of a particular relationship." In the meantime, the Court worked hard to clear up just what the establishment clause really means. Still later, in a 1971 case,** the Court said that every law or government policy must meet three tests. First, it must have a secular (nonreligious) purpose. Second, its main effect must neither help nor hurt religion. Finally, it must not cause the government to be excessively entangled, or involved, with religion. If the law or policy could meet all three tests—purpose, effect, and entanglement—the Court said it would not violate the establishment clause.

Now let's look at *Aguilar,* in which the three tests were applied to New York City's remedial education program. Justice Brennan, who wrote the opinion, admitted that the program had a secular purpose. This purpose was to help poor, educationally deprived schoolchildren, regardless of religion. He also agreed that the program neither hurt nor helped religion. As mentioned above, New York had made sure of this by assigning supervisors to drop in and check on the remedial teachers unannounced. However, said Justice Brennan, even though this supervision helped the program pass the second test, it made it fail the third test! He said the supervision was an "excessive entanglement" of public authorities with religious institutions.

WHAT IMPLICATIONS DO THESE CASES HAVE FOR THE FUTURE?

These two cases illustrate two different points in the development of the same view of the establishment clause. Yet their outcomes are completely different. Even some of the members of the Supreme Court say that the Court's decisions based on the establishment clause have zigzagged. Some members of the Court want to keep the purpose-effect-entanglement test as it is. Other members say they want to keep the test, but they would like to see some changes made in it. One member of the Court thinks that the test should be discarded completely. We cannot be sure what will happen in the future, but an important change in the Court's view of the establishment clause seems more and more likely.

BRAIN TEASERS

1. Why do you think that the Supreme Court decided that separation between church and state is more like a blurred line than a wall? Explain your reasoning.
2. In your own words, explain the three parts of the purpose-effect-entanglement test.
3. Remember that in *Aguilar v. Felton* what New York did to pass the second part of the purpose-effect-entanglement test was seen as making it fail the third part of the purpose-effect-entanglement test. Several members of the Court dissented angrily. They said that this ruling set up a no-win situation. Do you agree with the ruling or with the dissenters? Why?

---

* *Walz v. Tax Commission* ** *Lemon v. Kurtzman*

8. *REYNOLDS V. UNITED STATES* and *WISCONSIN V. YODER*
98 U.S. 145 (1879) and 406 U.S. 205 (1972)

WHAT WERE THESE CASES ABOUT?

The stories. Like the last two cases you studied, these two cases are about religion. But these cases concern a different part of the Constitution and raise very different issues.

Reynolds v. United States is a simple story. As in the states, the law in early Utah Territory made it a crime for a man to have more than one wife at the same time. This practice is called bigamy. However, Utah Territory had been settled mostly by members of the Church of Jesus Christ of Latter-Day Saints, called Mormons. At that time Mormons believed that God permitted men to have several wives. In fact, they thought that when circumstances permitted, marrying several wives was a religious duty. When a Mormon named George Reynolds was convicted of bigamy, he appealed, saying that his constitutional right to practice his religion had been taken away.

The story in *Wisconsin v. Yoder* is equally simple and very similar. Several communities of people who practice the Amish religion live in Wisconsin. The Amish believe that the world is ungodly and morally corrupt. To please God they separate their communities from the world as much as possible. For example, they do not want their children forced to attend public high schools, where they would be exposed to worldly influences that might tempt them to accept wrong beliefs and bad ways of life. But Wisconsin law requires children to be educated for a certain number of years. When Yoder and several other Amish parents kept their children out of high school, they were charged with violating the school attendance law. Convicted, they made the same appeal as Reynolds. The law, they protested, took away their constitutional right to practice their religion. They said that obeying the law would endanger their own salvation as well as the salvation of their children.

The questions. In each of these cases the defendants said that the laws under which they had been convicted violated the "free exercise clause" of the First Amendment.

Therefore, the questions in the two cases were almost identical. *Reynolds* asked if it was a violation of the free exercise clause to punish a person for breaking a bigamy law that goes against Mormon beliefs. *Yoder* asked if it was a violation of the free exercise clause to punish a person for breaking a school attendance law that goes against Amish beliefs.

The issues. If you read the First Amendment carefully, you will see that it says not just one thing about religion but two. Its wording is, "Congress shall make no law . . . respecting an establishment of religion, or prohibiting the free exercise thereof." You studied the establishment clause in the last two cases. The free exercise clause, though, adds a new dimension to the Supreme Court's cases.

A paraphrase of the free exercise clause might be "Congress is not allowed to make laws that stop people from freely practicing their religions." But just what does this clause mean? Surely it means that government should not stop people from believing what their religions teach. But perhaps it also means that government should not stop people from acting as their religions teach. The issue that the Court had to decide, then, was if the free exercise clause was not only about belief but also about action.

HOW WERE THE CASES DECIDED?

The results of the two cases before us were very different. In *Reynolds* the Supreme Court ruled that Utah Territory's bigamy law did not violate the free exercise right of Mormons. In *Yoder* it ruled that Wisconsin's school attendance law violated the free exercise right of the Amish.

WHAT DID THE COURT SAY ABOUT CONSTITUTIONAL RIGHTS?

Chief Justice Morrison Remick Waite wrote the Court's opinion in *Reynolds*. As you read, the issue the Court had to decide was if the free exercise clause is not just about belief but also about action. The chief justice's opinion was simple and clear: the free exercise clause is only about belief. So the fact that George Reynolds *believed* God wanted him to have several wives was not the state's concern. On the other hand, if he *acted* on that belief the government could punish him.

Some people objected that this opinion put the government above God. However, Chief Justice Waite had an answer to such an objection. He said that if the free exercise clause applied to action as well as belief then nothing at all could be forbidden. For instance, you know that it is against the law to commit murder. Somebody could say, "That law takes away my constitutional rights because my religion requires human sacrifice."

In *Yoder v. Wisconsin* Wisconsin authorities urged the Court to distinguish between belief and action just as former Chief Justice Waite had 100 years earlier. Then Yoder would have been in the wrong. Speaking for the Court, Chief Justice Warren Burger refused. At least in this case, he said, "belief and action cannot be confined in logic-tight compartments." Instead of reasoning like Chief Justice Waite, Chief Justice Burger followed up something that the Court had said in 1952.* The free exercise clause, it had remarked, shows that "we are a religious people whose institutions presuppose a Supreme Being. We make room for as wide a variety of beliefs and creeds as the spiritual needs of man make necessary." Chief Justice Burger thought this statement meant that wherever possible, the government should "accommodate," or allow for, the various ways of life in which people of different religions believe.

In his opinion Chief Justice Burger expressed a new principle. Let's look at the three parts of the principle. First, the actions that the government wants to forbid must be interfering with what the government is doing to achieve some purpose. Second, the government's purpose must be an extremely important one. Third, what the government is doing to achieve the purpose must be the only way it can be achieved. Now, let's apply this principle to *Wisconsin v. Yoder*:

- What purpose was the Wisconsin government trying to achieve? (To educate children well enough to play their roles as citizens)
- Was this purpose extremely important? (The chief justice agreed that it was.)
- How was Wisconsin trying to achieve it? (By making all children go to high school)
- But was this the only way the purpose could be achieved? (The chief justice said it was not. The Amish put their teenage children

---

* *Zorach v. Clauson*

to work in the community. In this way they "learned by doing." Chief Justice Burger said this type of education seemed to work well enough. For evidence he said that the Amish had shown themselves to be good citizens. Therefore, he said, the Constitution does not allow Wisconsin to force Amish parents to send their children to public high school.)

WHAT IMPLICATIONS DO THESE CASES HAVE FOR THE FUTURE?

First, you know that for future cases, the idea that the Constitution protects only religious belief and not religious action has been rejected. Second, you know that to decide when religious conduct must be accommodated and when it may be forbidden, the Supreme Court has a new principle.

Will the Court keep this new principle, or will it change its interpretation? We cannot predict the answer. We can, however, get some hints about the future by thinking about questions that the new principle does not answer. One such question is, "What is a religion?" Some members of the Supreme Court were very upset about Chief Justice Burger's opinion. They said he seemed to think that a **sect** counts as a religion only if its members are considered good citizens. This question will have to be faced sometime in the future.

Another clue that there may be a new interpretation is that the new principle uses the balancing test. To apply the principle, the court must balance the right to free exercise of religion against other important government purposes. As you read in the lesson on *Schenck v. United States*, balancing tests are controversial. Saying that a right must be balanced against other purposes means admitting that the right is not absolute. Some judges believe that if a right is not absolute, it is not really a right at all.

BRAIN TEASERS

1. What do you think the First Amendment means by the word *religion?* Explain your reasoning.
2. Do you agree with Chief Justice Burger that free exercise rights can be outweighed by extremely important government purposes (such as national security or protecting people from harm), or do you think nothing is important enough to outweigh free exercise rights? Support your answer.
3. Make a list of other religious practices that people might want the government to accommodate. Here are some examples to get you started: refusal to serve in the armed forces and refusal to work on the Sabbath. Imagine that you are the new chief justice of the Supreme Court. To each practice on your list, apply the principle developed by Chief Justice Burger in *Wisconsin v. Yoder.* Do you think that the government should accommodate the practice? Explain your reasoning.

9. *YOUNGSTOWN SHEET & TUBE COMPANY V. SAWYER*
343 U.S. 579 (1952)

WHAT WAS THIS CASE ABOUT?

The story. The time was 1952. Far away in Korea, American forces were at war. At home factories were working hard to supply them with weapons. However, labor and management in the steel industry were having a little "war" of their own. The time had come to negotiate a new contract between the steel companies and the steel workers' union. Even though negotiators from both sides had been meeting for weeks, they had been unable to agree. Twice the government tried to help the two sides come to an agreement, but still no contract was in sight. Frustrated, the union representatives set a deadline. They said that if no agreement was reached by midnight April 9, a nationwide strike would begin one minute later.

A few hours before the strike was to begin, President Truman ordered Commerce Secretary Charles S. Sawyer to take control of most of the steel mills and keep them running. Sawyer immediately issued orders to the steel companies. Troops were sent into the mills to take the workers' places. In the morning the president told Congress what he had done. Congress did not take any action. On several previous occasions when Congress had made laws about labor disputes, the idea of giving the president power to seize companies had been considered. It had always been rejected.

The steel companies obeyed the commerce secretary's orders, but they protested. Saying that neither Congress nor the Constitution gave the president power to seize the steel mills, they asked the courts to declare the orders of Truman and Sawyer invalid. Because the United States was in the midst of a war, the Supreme Court "cut some red tape" (skipped over normal procedures) and heard the case in a very early stage of legal proceedings.

The question. Justice Hugo Black wrote the Court's opinion. As he put it, the question before the Court was "Is the seizure order within the constitutional power of the president?"

The issues. Remember that in *McCulloch v. Maryland* the Court ruled that Congress has not only the powers that are explicitly listed in the Constitution but also powers that are needed to carry out the listed powers. President Truman and Secretary Sawyer made a similar claim. They admitted that in the part of the Constitution where the president's job is described, no power to seize industrial property is mentioned. But the Constitution does make the president the chief executive of the United States as well as commander in chief of the armed forces. Truman and Sawyer said that a broad power to deal with emergencies was included in the very idea of a chief executive as the armed forces commander in chief. Because *inherent* means "included in the very idea of," they called it an **inherent power.** They said that this inherent power included the power to seize industrial property in certain emergency situations. The Court had to decide if this line of reasoning was correct.

HOW WAS THE CASE DECIDED?

In an opinion written by Justice Black, six of the nine Justices ruled that the seizure order was unconstitutional and must be canceled.

WHAT DID THE COURT SAY ABOUT GOVERNMENTAL POWERS?

First, Justice Black said that the seizure of the mills could not be justified by the fact that the president is commander in chief of the armed forces. Truman and Sawyer had argued that courts often upheld broad powers for military commanders at the scene of battle. The Court said that even though a war was going on, the United States was not a scene of battle.

Second, Justice Black said that the seizure of the mills could not be justified by the president's job as chief executive. An executive is not a lawmaker. According to the Constitution, Congress is to make laws; the executive branch is to "execute" them, or carry them out. Whether or not seizure of industrial property is a good way to deal with labor disputes that stop production is a matter to be settled by law and not by executive action.

The president's order, Justice Black remarked, was written in much the same way that laws are written. He said, however, that being written like a law did not make it a law. "The president's order does not direct that a congressional policy be executed in a manner prescribed by Congress—it directs that a presidential policy be executed in a manner prescribed by Congress." The action could not be permitted.

WHAT IMPLICATIONS DOES THIS CASE HAVE FOR THE FUTURE?

Did you notice that the Court's opinion did not make a flat statement that there is no such thing as an inherent power? Asking whether there is any such thing is easy.

Answering the question, however, is not so easy. Each of the six justices in the majority reasoned in a slightly different way. Justice Black's opinion was very brief because it included only what all six could agree to. The reason he did not say that there is no such thing as an inherent power is that not all of the six justices were ready to agree.

One member of the majority, Justice Tom Campbell Clark, said that the Constitution gives the president broad power in times of deep national emergency, whether this power is called "inherent," "moral," "implied," "emergency," or something else. He thought that if Congress had never said anything about how emergencies are to be handled, the president would have had to use his own judgment. Clark believed the key fact was that Congress had said quite a bit about how emergencies are to be handled. Therefore, the president had been wrong to take the decision into his own hands. The three dissenting justices said that there is such a thing as an inherent power. They disagreed, however, with Justice Clark's view that it had not been properly used in this case.

The Court's argument against President Truman's seizure of the steel mills tells us something about the future. It demonstrates the Court's determination to uphold the separation of powers. Congress is to set policy; the president is to carry it out. The Court's inability to agree to a flat statement about whether or not there is such a thing as an inherent presidential power tells us something about the future. It tells us that until the Court can agree, this issue is likely to come up again and again in different kinds of situations.

BRAIN TEASERS

1. This case was started by the steel companies, so you know that management disapproved of the seizure order. How do you think the steel workers' union reacted to the seizure order? Why?
2. Remember why the Court said that President Truman's role as commander in chief of the armed forces did not justify the seizure order: the place where the seizures took place was not the scene of battle. How might Truman have replied to this argument?
3. How does this case illustrate our system of checks and balances?

10. PLESSY V. FERGUSON and BROWN V. BOARD OF EDUCATION
163 U.S. 537 (1896) and 347 U.S. 483 (1954)

WHAT WERE THESE CASES ABOUT?

The stories. These two cases illustrate a profound change in the legality of racial **segregation.**

Plessy v. Ferguson begins with a law passed by the Louisiana legislature in 1890. The law required all railway companies in the state to provide "separate but equal" accommodations for white and African American passengers. A group of people who did not think the law was fair recruited a young man named Homer Plessy to get arrested on purpose in order to test the law. Homer Plessy entered a train and took an empty seat in an all-white coach. The conductor tried to make him move to an all-black coach. When Plessy refused he was arrested by a police officer and put in jail. In his defense he said that the 1890 law was unconstitutional. The case eventually came to the United States Supreme Court and was decided in 1896.

More than 50 years later an African American named Oliver Brown moved with his family into a white neighborhood in Topeka, Kansas. The Browns assumed that their daughter, Linda, would attend the neighborhood school. Instead, the school board ordered her to attend a distant all-black school that was supposedly "separate but equal." Saying that school segregation violated the 14th Amendment to the Constitution, Mr. Brown sued the school board. He asked the courts to order that his daughter be permitted to attend the neighborhood school. Similar cases were developing in South Carolina, Virginia, and Delaware. The Supreme Court's decision in *Brown v. Board of Education* settled all four cases at once.

The question. The question raised by the Court was the same in both cases. In one case the question was applied to transportation while in the other it was applied to public education. That question was: Do racially segregated facilities violate the "equal protection" clause of the 14th Amendment?

The issues. The 14th Amendment is one of several amendments that were passed soon after the Civil War to guarantee the freedom of African Americans and to protect them from unfair treatment. The wording of the equal protection clause is: "No State shall . . . deny to any person within its jurisdiction the equal protection of the laws." But just what does this wording forbid? Louisiana authorities in *Plessy* said that it did not forbid racial segregation in railway carriages. They argued that separate railway carriages for African Americans and whites could be equal. For instance, they could be equally clean and equally safe. Kansas authorities in *Brown* said much the same thing. They claimed that their all-black and all-white schools were equal in the skill of their teachers, the quality of their buildings, and so on.

In the days of racial segregation the claim that segregated facilities were equal in tangible, or measurable, features was almost always a terrible lie. Railroad companies would reserve only the oldest and most worn cars for African Americans. School boards often would spend three times as much money for each white student as for each African American student. But the issue facing the Court went much deeper. Even if things were made equal in racially segregated facilities, was that enough to satisfy the requirement for "equal protection of the laws"? Or was there something inherently unequal about segregation?

HOW WERE THE CASES DECIDED?

In *Plessy v. Ferguson,* decided in 1896, the Court ruled that the 14th Amendment's equal protection clause allows racial segregation. In *Brown v. Board of Education,* decided in 1954, the Court unanimously reversed course, ruling that the equal protection clause does not allow racial segregation.

WHAT DID THE COURT SAY ABOUT CONSTITUTIONAL RIGHTS?

Justice Henry Billings Brown wrote the Court's opinion in *Plessy*. He admitted that the purpose of the 14th Amendment was "to enforce the absolute equality of the two races before the law." But then he said that this statement meant political equality, not social equality. In his view, neither African Americans nor white people wanted the races to mingle. He knew that an objection to his position could be made. Somebody might say that even if the facilities offered to African Americans and whites were equal, separation of the races themselves implied that African Americans were inferior to whites. However, Justice Brown said that this objection was a "fallacy," or false belief. If any African American people thought enforced racial segregation stamped them with a "badge of inferiority," he said, the fault was not in the law but in their attitude.

In *Brown* the Court's opinion was written by Chief Justice Earl Warren. It is as different from the *Plessy* opinion as night is from day. Separation of African American schoolchildren from white schoolchildren of the same

age and ability, he said, "generates a feeling of inferiority as to their status in the community that may affect their hearts and minds in a way unlikely ever to be undone." He said that when racial segregation is required by law, the harm is even greater. It makes no difference that "the physical facilities and other 'tangible' factors may be equal," he said. The inequality is inherent in racial segregation itself. Enforced separation of the races in public education is unconstitutional. It is not equal protection and never can be equal protection.

WHAT IMPLICATIONS DID THESE CASES HAVE FOR THE FUTURE?

In *Brown v. Board of Education* the Court did not say that the "separate but equal" doctrine had no place anywhere. It said that the "separate but equal" doctrine had no place "in the field of public education." Even though this statement was limited, it had a powerful impact on future cases. Today, no judge would ever suggest that what is "separate" can be "equal." *Plessy v. Ferguson* has been completely discarded.

Taken together, *Plessy* and *Brown* show the moral power of protest as well as the flexibility of the Constitution. The Constitution contains legal principles whose interpretations may change as American society changes. The decision in *Plessy* was not unanimous. An emotional dissenting opinion was written by Justice John Marshall Harlan. Even though Justice Harlan came from a family that had once owned slaves, he had come to understand the evil of enforced racial segregation. "What can more certainly arouse race hate, what more certainly create and perpetuate a feeling of distrust between the races," he asked, than laws that assume that African American people are inferior. In words that ring like a liberty bell, he said that "in the view of the Constitution, in the eye of the law, there is in this country no superior, dominant, ruling class of citizens. There is no caste here. Our Constitution is color-blind, and neither knows nor tolerates classes among its citizens."

It took more than 50 years, but eventually Justice Harlan's dissent became the law of the land.

1. In 1896 Justice Harlan said that enforced racial segregation was unequal even when the public facilities provided for African Americans and whites were the same. In 1954 the entire Supreme Court said the same thing. Explain their arguments in your own words.

2. Justice Brown seemed to think that enforced racial segregation *reflected* certain feelings African Americans and whites had for each other. Justice Harlan, by contrast, thought that enforced racial segregation would *cause* African Americans and whites to have certain feelings for each other. Think about this disagreement, and then explain what you think it means.

11. *LOVING V. VIRGINIA*
388 U.S. 1 (1967)

WHAT WAS THIS CASE ABOUT?

The story. As late as the 1960s, 16 states had laws that forbade and punished marriages between people of different races. One of these states was Virginia. The Virginia law banned all interracial marriages in which one of the partners was white. For instance, a marriage between an African American and a Cherokee Indian would have been legal.

Yet it is hard to tell people with whom to fall in love. This case is about the Lovings, an African American woman and a white man. Because they lived in Virginia, they had to travel to the District of Columbia to get married. When they returned to Virginia to live, they were arrested. The Virginia court rejected their claim that the law was wrong. Unwilling to give up, Mr. and Mrs. Loving appealed to the federal courts, saying that the Virginia law violated the 14th Amendment. Their case was decided by the Supreme Court in 1967.

The question. Did Virginia's law against certain kinds of interracial marriages violate the 14th Amendment?

The issues. The meanings of two different clauses of the 14th Amendment were argued in this case. You have learned about both of these clauses in previous lessons: the equal protection clause and the due process clause.

To prove that the Virginia law deprived citizens of equal protection, it would not be enough to point out that the law classified citizens according to race. The Court would have to look at the reason for this racial classification. Was the reason to put people of one race above another? For instance, suppose scientists discover a new disease that attacks only white-skinned people, and researchers have developed a shot that keeps people from getting the disease. Virginia might pass a law requiring white-skinned schoolchildren to get the shot but not requiring other schoolchildren to get it. Obviously, this law classifies citizens by race. However, its purpose is not to put one race above another. Therefore, this law would not violate the equal protection clause.

Now remember the wording of the due process clause. It says that no state may take away its citizens' life, liberty, or property without due process of law. The issue here is which freedoms are included in the word *liberty*. In order to prove that the Virginia law violated the due process clause, it would not be enough to point out that it took away the freedom to marry a person of one's choice. The Court would have to consider whether or not this is one of the liberties to which the due process clause refers. For instance, suppose Virginia passes a law that imposes severe punishments for driving a car while under the influence of alcohol. Obviously, this law takes away the freedom to engage in drunken driving. However, drunken driving is not one of the liberties to which the due process clause refers. Therefore, this law would not violate the due process clause.

HOW WAS THE CASE DECIDED?

In an opinion written by Chief Justice Earl Warren, the Supreme Court unanimously ruled that Virginia's law against interracial marriages violated the 14th Amendment.

WHAT DID THE COURT SAY ABOUT CONSTITUTIONAL RIGHTS?

Remember that in order to decide if the Virginia law violated the equal protection clause, the Supreme Court had to look at the reasons for the law. These reasons were not hard to find because they had been stated, and defended, by the Virginia state court. They were to "preserve the racial integrity" of Virginia citizens, and prevent the "corruption of blood" and the "obliteration of racial pride." Chief Justice Warren said that these statements were "obviously an endorsement of White Supremacy." Another fact demonstrating that Virginia wanted to put whites above people of other races was that its law did not punish all interracial marriages but only interracial marriages involving whites. Putting one race above another is exactly the kind of purpose the equal protection clause was meant to prevent.

Now remember that in order to decide whether the Virginia law violated the due process clause, the Supreme Court had to decide whether or not freedom to marry a person of one's choice is one of the liberties to which the clause refers. Chief Justice Warren said that it was. "Marriage," he insisted, "is one of the 'basic civil rights of man.'" Surely, he said, to take away this "fundamental freedom" for such a flimsy reason as a racial classification violates the promise of due process of law.

WHAT IMPLICATIONS DOES THIS CASE HAVE FOR THE FUTURE?

The most obvious thing that this case illustrates is the Court's determination to wipe out every trace of racial discrimination in the laws. In this way it continued the revolution begun in *Brown v. Board of Education.*

However, that is not all the case tells us about the future. The case deals not only with race but with marriage. State marriage laws often include various kinds of restrictions on who may marry. Restriction according to race, obviously, is now ruled out. But what about other kinds of restrictions? When the Court called marriage a "basic civil right of man" and a "fundamental freedom," it did not mean that no other kinds of restrictions could stand. However, using this language was a hint that if other kinds of restrictions are challenged in the courts, states will have to present very good reasons for them.

BRAIN TEASERS

1. What is the main purpose of the equal protection clause? How was the equal protection clause used in this case?

2. When the Court called marriage a "basic civil right of man" and a "fundamental freedom," it did not mean that no limitations on who may marry could stand. Can you think of any limitations on who may marry for which a good reason can be given? Explain your answer.

3. What other "fundamental freedoms" do you think the due process clause might protect? Why?

12. *GIDEON V. WAINWRIGHT*
372 U.S. 436 (1963)

WHAT WAS THIS CASE ABOUT?

The story. Clarence Earl Gideon was accused of breaking and entering into a Florida poolroom and stealing. The theft in this case was minor, but breaking and entering is a major crime. When Gideon's case came to trial he could not afford to hire a lawyer, and he asked that the court supply him with one for free. The judge refused. Gideon did his best to conduct his own defense, but he was found guilty. While he was in prison, Gideon spent hours studying law books. Using only what he learned in the law books, he wrote a legal document, called a **writ,** asking the United States Supreme Court to review his case. He claimed that by refusing to appoint a lawyer to help him, the Florida court had violated rights promised him by the Sixth and 14th Amendments. The Court issued its ruling in 1963.

The question. Is it a violation of the Sixth or 14th Amendment to deny a poor person accused of a major crime the free assistance of a lawyer?

The issues. The Sixth Amendment promises certain rights to people accused of crimes. One of the promises is that "the accused shall enjoy the right . . . to have the Assistance of Counsel [a lawyer] for his defense." By itself this amendment applies only to people on trial in federal courts. Thus, federal law required that poor people be provided with free lawyers in federal trials. That law did not help Gideon, however. He was accused of breaking state laws, so he was tried in a state court. Here is where the 14th Amendment comes in. As you remember, the 14th Amendment promises that states will not deprive people of life, liberty, or property without due process of law. Gideon had certainly been deprived of liberty because he had been put in jail. Had this liberty been taken away without due process of law? The answer depends on the meaning of "due process of law."

HOW WAS THE CASE DECIDED?

In a unanimous opinion written by Justice Hugo Black, the Court ruled in Gideon's favor.

WHAT DID THE COURT SAY ABOUT CONSTITUTIONAL RIGHTS?

Two different views of the Court explain why the 14th Amendment requires the appointment of lawyers for people too poor to hire lawyers themselves. One is the **incorporation view.** Justices who take this view think that the purpose of the due process clause is to take the first eight amendments in the Bill of Rights, which previously applied only to the federal government, and apply them to the states. In other words, the first eight amendments in the Bill of Rights would be incorporated into state court procedures. The second is the **fundamental liberties view.** Justices who take this view believe that "due process of law" means "whatever is necessary for justice." They think that what is necessary for justice may not include every promise in the first eight amendments. But they also believe that what is necessary for justice may include promises that go beyond anything in the first eight amendments. In *Gideon v. Wainwright* the justices came to the same conclusion about what should be done even though they held different views about the 14th Amendment.

Justice Black, who wrote the Court's opinion in *Gideon,* believed in the incorporation view. However, because he was writing for all nine justices, he had to take their opinions into account. Not all of them accepted the incorporation view. Thus, the opinion was a compromise. It included only general statements that would be acceptable to justices holding either view. The opinion said that the Sixth Amendment's promise of the "assistance of counsel" is necessary for a fair trial in any court. It did not say, however, that every other promise in the first eight amendments is also covered by the due process clause.

WHAT IMPLICATIONS DOES THIS CASE HAVE FOR THE FUTURE?

The first attempt to give free legal help to the poor was in 1876, when a group of German Americans formed a committee to give legal assistance to poor people. Such legal aid societies were quite successful. At first, they usually had too little money and too few volunteers to handle many criminal cases. *Gideon v. Wainwright* was one of several key Supreme Court cases guaranteeing that the government would pay lawyers to help poor people accused of crimes. A landmark law that provided such funding was the Criminal Justice Act of 1964, signed into law the year after the *Gideon* decision. Today, a few states have public defender programs with lawyers who receive a state salary to assist poor defendants. However, this is expensive. In most states lawyers for the poor are appointed by judges and paid by the state on a case-by-case basis. As you can see, *Gideon* is part of a long development in the assistance of poor people who are accused of crimes. This development is still going on.

| BRAIN TEASERS |

1. Carefully read all of the promises made in the first eight amendments to the Constitution. Make a list of the rights that are guaranteed in civil or criminal trials.
2. Now go over your list. Remember that originally, these promises only protected people from action by the federal government. Can you find any that, in your opinion, are not needed to protect people against state governments? Support your answer.
3. Does your list include everything necessary to guarantee justice in civil and criminal trials or should some promises be added? Explain your reasoning.

13. *MIRANDA V. ARIZONA*
384 U.S. 436 (1966)

WHAT WAS THIS CASE ABOUT?

The story. On March 13, 1963, an 18-year-old woman was kidnapped near Phoenix, Arizona. A few days later Ernesto Miranda was arrested for the crime and taken to the police station. He was 23 years old, lived in poverty, and had a limited education.

At the police station the victim picked out Ernesto Miranda from a lineup. Two officers then took him to a room to question him. Although at first Miranda denied the crime, after a short time he gave a detailed oral confession. He then made a written confession, which he signed.

At Miranda's trial the two officers testified that they had warned Miranda that anything he might say could be used against him in court and that Miranda had understood. The officers also said that he had given the confessions without any threats or force. They admitted, however, that they had not told Miranda about his right to silence or legal assistance. Miranda was found guilty and sentenced to a long prison term. After his conviction was upheld by the Arizona Supreme Court, Miranda appealed to the United States Supreme Court. He said that by neglecting to inform him of his rights to silence and to a lawyer, the police had violated rights promised to him by the Fifth, Sixth, and 14th Amendments.

The question. Is it a violation of the Fifth, Sixth, or 14th Amendment to use a confession from a person who has not been informed of his or her constitutional rights to silence and legal assistance?

The issues. You have already read that the Sixth Amendment promises the assistance of a lawyer in federal courts to people accused of crimes and that the 14th Amendment applies this promise to the states. Another promise about the way trials are conducted is given in the Fifth Amendment. It says: "No person . . . shall be compelled [forced] in any criminal case to be a witness against himself. . . ." For a person to be a "witness against himself" means to give information that shows he or she is guilty. The Fifth Amendment gives a person the right to refuse to give such information—to be silent. Without such a right, innocent people could be tortured until they confessed to crimes that they did not commit.

One issue in the *Miranda* case was when a person's Fifth and Sixth Amendment rights begin. Do they begin only at the trial? Perhaps you have heard news reports about witnesses answering courtroom questions by saying, "I take my Fifth Amendment right to

remain silent." Or do these rights begin earlier, in the police station, or even at the scene of arrest?

An even deeper issue concerns the meaning of being forced to be a witness against oneself. You already know that Miranda was not tortured or threatened. But there might be other ways of forcing or compelling a person to give information. What other ways are there? Perhaps keeping a person ignorant about his or her rights should count as a kind of force. Miranda was not told that he had a right to silence or legal assistance. Perhaps he thought that he had to speak. Perhaps, thinking that he was helpless, he was afraid. Perhaps letting a frightened person think that he or she has to speak is just like forcing him or her to speak. If so, then it violates the Fifth Amendment. Does this line of reasoning make sense? That question was the second issue the Court had to solve.

HOW WAS THE CASE DECIDED?

By only a five to four majority, the Supreme Court ruled that taking Miranda's confession without informing him of his rights to silence and legal assistance had deprived him of these rights.

WHAT DID THE COURT SAY ABOUT CONSTITUTIONAL RIGHTS?

The first issue facing the Court was when an accused person's Fifth and Sixth Amendment rights begin. The Court's view was that they begin as soon as the person is arrested. The second issue was whether or not failing to inform the accused person of his or her rights counts as a violation of these rights. The Court said that it does.

Today, in the very next breath after saying, "You are under arrest," a police officer reads a prisoner the *Miranda* warning. The word *read* is used because in many police departments police officers are given cards with prisoners' constitutional rights written on them. Officers read the rights so that they cannot later be faulted for misstating any of the rights. In many places the accused must sign the card, showing he or she is aware of and understands his or her rights. For people who don't speak or understand English, the whole process is done in their native language. The word *warning* is used because prisoners are warned that anything they say may be used against them.

The Miranda Warnings

1. You have the right to have a lawyer present to advise you prior to and during any questioning; and
2. If you are unable to employ a lawyer, you have the right to have a lawyer appointed to advise you prior to and during any questioning; and
3. You have the right to remain silent and not make any statement at all and any statement you make may be used against you at your trial; and
4. Any statement you make may be used as evidence against you in court; and
5. You have the right to terminate the interview at any time.

Source: Austin, Texas, Police Department

If prisoners are not informed of their rights, then judges will rule that what they tell the police may not be used as evidence against them in court, nor can any evidence police find that was based on what the prisoner said. The arrest may still be valid, however. It is only the accused person's statements that cannot be used as evidence if the Miranda warning has not been read. Other evidence may be used in court, and in fact, at his second trial, Miranda was convicted on other evidence.

According to the Supreme Court, people can give up the rights to silence and legal assistance, but only if they do so voluntarily, knowingly, and intelligently. The Court also declared that people do not give up their right to silence simply by starting to answer questions. They may begin to answer questions but then change their minds and refuse to say anything more until a lawyer arrives.

WHAT IMPLICATIONS DOES THIS CASE HAVE FOR THE FUTURE?

Miranda v. Arizona has been one of the most controversial cases in the history of the Supreme Court. Even the members of the Court split five to four. Indeed, just as some members of the Court thought the Court had gone too far, other members thought it had not gone far enough.

Among the general public the most hotly debated aspect of the Court's decision has been the rule that confessions given by prisoners who have not been informed of their rights may not be used as evidence in trials. The Court made this rule to prevent innocent people from being found guilty. Some people accept this reasoning. Others think that the rule prevents guilty people from being found guilty. They think it makes a police officer's job more difficult. *Miranda* demonstrates the delicate balance between protecting the accused and protecting society.

BRAIN TEASERS

1. Write two paragraphs. In the first paragraph defend the view that "The *Miranda* rule prevents innocent people from being found guilty." In the second paragraph defend the view that "The *Miranda* rule prevents guilty people from being found guilty." Try to anticipate what you think the opposing arguments would be and respond to those arguments.
2. Some people say that both statements are true—that the Miranda rule prevents innocent people from being found guilty and that it prevents guilty people from being found guilty. How much weight do you think should each goal be given—the goal of freeing innocent people and the goal of convicting guilty ones? Explain your reasoning.

14. TINKER V. DES MOINES INDEPENDENT COMMUNITY SCHOOL DISTRICT
393 U.S. 503 (1969)

WHAT WAS THIS CASE ABOUT?

The story. During the Vietnam War a group of adults and students in Des Moines, Iowa, planned a protest to the war. They decided to wear black armbands to show that they were against the war. When members of the Des Moines school board heard of the plan, most of them were deeply concerned. They held a meeting and decided to adopt a policy stating that any student who wore an armband to school would be asked to remove it. If students refused, they would be suspended from school until they were willing to come back without the armbands.

On December 16, 1965, Mary Beth Tinker and her older brother, John Tinker, wore black armbands to their schools. Chris Eckhardt wore an armband on the following day. All three students were suspended from school. Eventually, they did return to school without the armbands. However, they said that their First Amendment right to freedom of speech had been violated. They asked the United States District Court to order school authorities to reverse the suspensions. In 1969 the case was decided by the United States Supreme Court.

The question. Is it a violation of the First Amendment promise of freedom of speech for school officials to prohibit students from wearing armbands to symbolize political protest?

The issues. The Court had to work through several difficult questions. It had to decide if wearing an armband symbolizing political protest was the same as speech. The protest did not involve spoken words, but it did express an opinion. The court had to decide if expression was protected in the same way that speech was.

Another question was if it made any difference that Mary Beth, John, and Chris chose to wear the armbands in school rather than somewhere else. This question arose because of what the Court had said in previous cases. It had declared that the promise of free speech does not mean that one may speak anywhere, at any time, or in any way. Des Moines school officials thought that school was the wrong place for an antiwar protest. They said that the protest would disrupt teaching and learning.

Finally, the Court faced the question of whether or not teenagers have the same rights to speech that adults do. Teenagers are citizens, but some rights, such as voting, are reserved for adult citizens.

HOW WAS THE CASE DECIDED?

By a large majority, the justices of the Supreme Court ruled that the suspension from school of Mary Beth, John, and Chris was unconstitutional.

WHAT DID THE COURT SAY ABOUT CONSTITUTIONAL RIGHTS?

Remember that one question for the Court was if expression, such as wearing an armband, was the same as speech. The majority of the justices thought that there was a difference between "pure speech" and behavior that resembled speech. However, they said that wearing the armband was so much like pure speech that the First Amendment protected it just as fully.

Another question was if it made any difference that the students wore their armbands in school rather than someplace else. "It can hardly be argued," said the majority, "that either students or teachers shed their constitutional rights to freedom of speech or expression at the schoolhouse gate." They agreed that action that resembled speech could be punished if it really disrupted education. However, they accused the Des Moines officials of saying that they feared disruption when what they really feared was controversy.

The third question was if teenagers have the same rights to speech as adults. Surprisingly, the Court said nothing about this at all.

WHAT IMPLICATIONS DOES THIS CASE HAVE FOR THE FUTURE?

As you know, when new cases come before the Supreme Court, the members try to settle them by using the same principles that have been developed in earlier cases. What principles does this case express?

- The closer that an action resembling speech is to pure speech, the more freedom the First Amendment gives it.
- High schools are not "off limits" for free speech. In fact, the Court said that the communication of political opinions between students is an important part of the educational process.
- Student action that resembles speech can be punished but only if it really disrupts education.

We can also make some guesses about the future by looking at what the Court did *not* say. Issues that the Court did not settle might have to be faced again in the future.

- The Court said very little about how to tell which kinds of actions that resemble speech are enough like pure speech to deserve complete freedom.

- Moreover, it said nothing at all about whether the constitutional rights of teenage citizens are as full as those of adults.

Finally, we can glimpse the future by considering the opinions of the justices who wrote separate opinions. Even though the Court tries to use the same principles over and over, sometimes its members change their minds about controversial issues. An opinion expressed by only one justice today might become the opinion of the majority 10 years later.

Justice Potter Stewart, for instance, agreed with much of what was said by the majority. He also accepted their view that the Des Moines school authorities had acted unconstitutionally. However, he said, "I cannot share the Court's uncritical assumption that, school discipline aside, the First Amendment rights of children are coextensive with [extend as far as] adults." How far do the rights of teenagers extend? Justice Stewart thought that the Court should have faced this question instead of dodging it.

Justice Hugo Black did not accept the decision of the Court at all. He thought that the majority was wrong to rule that the Des Moines school officials had acted unconstitutionally. Justice Black and the majority agreed that disruption of the educational process would be a good reason to limit rights to speech in schools. But while the majority of justices did not think that the armband protest disrupted education, Justice Black said, "I think the record overwhelmingly shows that the armbands did exactly what the elected school officials and principals foresaw it would, that is, took the students' minds off their classwork and diverted them to thoughts about the highly emotional subject of the Vietnam War." The question of what is really disruptive and what is not will probably continue to divide the Court.

BRAIN TEASERS

1. What did you think about the Des Moines school board's action when you read *What Was This Case About?* Did you change your mind as you read the rest of the lesson? Why or why not?

2. The majority of the Court took it for granted that controversy alone does not count as a disruption of the educational process. Why not? Justice Black disagreed. Why?

3. The students in this case wore armbands to symbolize protest. Use your imagination to make a list of other acts that express opinions without the use of words. Which ones should be given the same freedom as pure speech? Which ones should not? Explain your reasoning.

4. Should teenagers have as much freedom of speech as adults? If you think so, explain why. If you don't think so, give examples of speech that should be permitted to adults but not to teenagers and explain your reasoning.

15. *ROE V. WADE*
410 U.S. 113 (1973)

WHAT WAS THIS CASE ABOUT?

The story. In 1970, Norma McCorvey, an unmarried pregnant woman living in Texas, sought to obtain a legal abortion in a medical facility. At that time, most states had very restrictive laws concerning the availability of abortions. Because of Texas antiabortion statutes, no licensed physician would agree to perform the abortion for Roe. Because she was financially unable to travel to another state with less-restrictive laws regulating abortions, Roe faced either continuing an unwanted pregnancy or having the procedure performed in a nonmedical facility, which, she believed, would endanger her life.

Roe claimed that the Texas antiabortion laws were unconstitutional in that they interfered with her right of personal privacy that is protected by the Ninth and 14th Amendments. She decided to take legal action, naming in her lawsuit Henry Wade, then the district attorney of Dallas County, Texas. Throughout the case, Norma McCorvey used the pseudonym of Jane Roe. The case was presented to the Supreme Court in December 1971. It was reargued in October 1972 and decided on January 22, 1973.

The question. Is it a violation of a person's right to privacy for a state to prevent a woman from terminating a pregnancy through an abortion?

The issues. The 14th Amendment says that "No state shall make or enforce any law which shall abridge the privileges . . . of citizens of the United States . . . nor deny to any person . . . the equal protection of the laws." The Ninth Amendment states that "The enumeration in the Constitution of certain rights shall not be construed to deny or disparage others retained by the people." Do these amendments encompass and protect a woman's right to a legal abortion?

HOW WAS THE CASE DECIDED?

In an opinion written by Justice Harry Blackmun, the Court ruled that the 14th Amendment's due process guarantee of personal liberty guarantees the right to personal privacy. This guarantee protects a woman's decision whether or not to continue a pregnancy and assures that a state's laws do not abridge, or diminish, this right. The vote was seven to two, with Chief Justice William Rehnquist and Justice Byron White dissenting.

WHAT DID THE COURT SAY ABOUT CONSTITUTIONAL RIGHTS?

In ruling that a state cannot prevent a woman from terminating a pregnancy during the first three months, the Court relied on citizens' right of privacy. Justice Blackmun stated in his opinion that "This right of privacy, whether it be founded in the Fourteenth Amendment's concept of personal liberty and restrictions upon state action, as we feel it is, or . . . in the Ninth Amendment's reservation of rights to the people, is broad enough to encompass a woman's decision whether or not to terminate her pregnancy." In its ruling, however, the Court recognized the right of a state to regulate abortions as a pregnancy progressed. Justice Blackmun divided pregnancy into three trimesters:

- During the first trimester, or first three months, of a pregnancy, a woman has an unrestricted right to an abortion, although a state can prevent abortions performed by nonphysicians.
- During the second trimester, a state can regulate abortions to protect a woman's health.

- Only in the third trimester, or final three months, of a pregnancy can a state forbid an abortion, unless it is necessary to protect a woman's health.

The ruling also said that a state cannot, on its own, adopt a theory of when life begins. This prevents a state from giving a fetus the same rights as a newborn child.

In 1965, the Court had considered the constitutional right to privacy in *Griswold v. Connecticut*, in which it ruled that restrictions on the availability of contraceptives violated this right. The right to privacy—the basis for the Court's ruling in *Roe v. Wade*—thus became a pivotal issue in cases that challenged abortion laws.

WHAT IMPLICATIONS DOES THIS CASE HAVE FOR THE FUTURE?

In his dissent, Chief Justice Rehnquist wrote, "The Court's opinion will accomplish the seemingly impossible feat of leaving this area of the law more confused than it found it." Today, *Roe v. Wade* is well known as the case that legalized abortion in the United States.

In the decades following the ruling, related cases have been decided that some people claim weaken the legislative impact of *Roe v. Wade*. In *Harris v. McRae* (1980), the Court ruled that the federal and local governments did not have to pay for abortions for women on welfare, even if the abortions were necessary for medical reasons. Critics of this ruling claimed that women who could not afford the procedure would, like Jane Roe, be faced with either continuing an unwanted pregnancy or resorting to dangerous measures to terminate it. Thus far, efforts to overturn *Roe v. Wade* have been unsuccessful. The strongest threat to the ruling has been *Webster v. Reproductive Health Services* (1989), which added more restrictions on the availability of abortions.

BRAIN TEASERS

1. Some legal experts contend that gender discrimination, rather than right to privacy, should have been the grounds of the Supreme Court's opinion in *Roe v. Wade*. For example, many abortion supporters argue that a woman has a constitutional right to make decisions regarding her own

body. In a paragraph, explain whether you agree or disagree with this argument.

2. Explain the importance of the Ninth and 14th Amendments to the Supreme Court's ruling in *Roe v. Wade*.

16. *UNITED STATES V. NIXON*
418 U.S. 683 (1974)

WHAT WAS THIS CASE ABOUT?

The story. It was late at night on June 17, 1972. In most of the nation's capital people were sleeping. In the Watergate Hotel five burglars were breaking into the headquarters of the Democratic National Committee. Their criminal mission was to photograph the Democratic party's plans for the upcoming presidential campaign and to install "bugs" for listening in on the Democratic party's telephone conversations. The burglars were caught in the act. One of them turned out to be an employee of President Richard Nixon's campaign organization, called the Committee to Re-elect the President. Investigation showed that two other Republican campaign officials were also involved.

When the president denied that anyone at the White House had known about the burglary, most people believed him. After his re-election, however, investigators uncovered additional information. Important members of the Nixon administration *had* known about the burglary after all. In a massive cover-up, they had even destroyed evidence! Most shocking of all, the president's lawyer, John Dean, testified before the Senate that the president had helped plan the cover-up from the beginning.

Could this be true? When Nixon denied it, investigators were stumped. But then another witness revealed that Nixon had secretly tape-recorded every conversation that had ever taken place in his office. The tapes would show whether or not Nixon was telling the truth.

By April 1974 criminal charges had been filed against seven members of the Nixon administration. Though Nixon was not charged, he was listed in the case as one of the people involved in the conspiracy. The special prosecutor in charge of the case at the time, Leon Jaworski, asked Nixon to let him hear the tapes. Nixon had already ordered a previous special prosecutor fired for asking the same thing, and to no one's surprise, Nixon refused again. However, Jaworski persisted. He asked the federal district court for help. When the judge ordered Nixon to release the tapes to the court for secret examination, Nixon disobeyed.

Refusing the special prosecutor's request caused a scandal, but disobeying the judge's order caused much more than a scandal. It caused a constitutional crisis—a tug of war between two branches of government. Could a president defy a federal judge?

Nixon claimed that he could. As president, he said, he had an **executive privilege** of keeping presidential communications confidential. He also said that the privilege was absolute, which meant that nobody could override it for any reason. Because of the urgency of the case, the United States Supreme Court agreed to skip over the Court of Appeals in order to settle the case right away.

The question. Does the Constitution give the president an absolute executive privilege?

The issues. President Nixon gave two arguments for his position. His first argument was that the principle of separation of powers requires that the executive and judicial branches be totally independent of each other. If presidents had to obey judges who ordered them to release evidence, this independence would be destroyed.

His second argument was that the secrecy of communications between a president and his advisers is necessary for the president to be able to look after the public good. Nixon said that if a president's advisers know that anything they said could be repeated to the public, they might worry too much about what people would think, and they would not give him good advice. Nixon said that if a president didn't receive good advice, it would be harder for him or her to carry out the presidency as spelled out in the Constitution.

HOW WAS THE CASE DECIDED?

In a decision written by Chief Justice Warren Burger, the Court ruled that the president's executive privilege is not absolute and that

Nixon had to turn over the recorded tapes as he had been ordered.

WHAT DID THE COURT SAY ABOUT GOVERNMENTAL POWERS?

The Court examined each of the president's two arguments in turn. One, you remember, was that preservation of the separation of powers requires the executive and judicial branches to be totally independent. Total independence means that the president does not have to obey court orders to release evidence. The chief justice rejected this claim. The Constitution is based on separation of powers, but under this separation it gives each power or branch a job of its own to do. If the president could withhold evidence from the courts, the courts could not do the job the Constitution gave them. "The powers," concluded the chief justice, "were not intended to operate with absolute independence."

Nixon's second argument was that communications between the president and his advisers need to be confidential for the sake of the public good. Chief Justice Burger admitted that sometimes confidentiality, or secretiveness, is important. But it only applies in specific instance. When communications are about diplomatic or military secrets, confidentiality is of the utmost importance. On the other hand, when communications concern other subjects, confidentiality might not be important at all. The chief justice concluded that in presidential claims of executive privilege, the need for confidentiality must be balanced against competing needs on a case-by-case basis.

Now, how does this idea help settle the case at hand? With what other need or needs did confidentiality compete in *United States v. Nixon?* It competed with the need to find out the truth in a criminal trial. The purpose of criminal justice, said Chief Justice Burger, "is that guilt not escape or innocence suffer." But finding out the truth in a criminal trial requires that courts have all the evidence they need, even if it includes presidential communications. In this case the courts needed the information on the tapes to carry out their duty. When the need to find out the truth in the Watergate trial was weighed against President Nixon's need for confidentiality, confidentiality lost. Confidentiality might have won had the tapes been about

diplomatic or military secrets or had they not contained crucial evidence. Moreover, the district court had not even planned to make the complete tapes public. It had planned to examine them in secret first. Only the parts that were necessary for the trial would be used in open court.

WHAT IMPLICATIONS DOES THIS CASE HAVE FOR THE FUTURE?

If the president had defied the Supreme Court as he had defied the district court, it would have been an important sign for the future. One reason is that the courts have no enforcement powers of their own. They depend on the executive branch to enforce their orders. If the executive branch defies a court order, the courts have no recourse. Another reason is that successful defiance of the Supreme Court would call the entire idea of judicial review into question. The judicial branch is the final judge of the meaning of the Constitution. Defiance by the president would be like saying that the executive branch is its own final judge.

Nixon did not defy the Supreme Court. He obeyed, not out of respect for judicial review, but out of self-interest. He feared that unless he gave in, the Senate would remove him from office. Even so, the evidence of the tapes turned out to be so damaging that Nixon felt he had to resign or the House would start impeachment proceedings. The tapes showed that he had been part of the cover-up.

What principles emerge from this case? The Court did not say whether or not such a thing as executive privilege exists. However, it clearly stated that there is no such thing as an absolute executive privilege. The Court put forth the following principles:

- The president's need for confidentiality must be weighed against competing needs, such as the needs of the criminal justice system.
- In disputed cases this weighing may be done by the federal courts.

Conflicts over executive privilege will probably continue to arise. Presidents have claimed executive privilege over 50 times just since 1952. In most of these cases they claimed the privilege in order to avoid giving Congress information that it had requested. So long as the two main principles listed above are accepted by all parties, these conflicts have much less chance of hurting the nation. The final decision is made by the judicial branch.

BRAIN TEASERS

The Constitution gives both the president and Congress important responsibilities for foreign policy. In Congress most of the weightiest responsibilities are given to the Senate. Use your imagination to make up a story about a conflict in which the Senate requests key foreign-policy documents, but the president claims executive privilege.

In your story:
a. Explain exactly what documents the Senate wants and why it wants them.
b. Explain why the president wants to keep the documents confidential.
c. Have the conflict settled by the Supreme Court. Tell what decision the court hands down and explain the basis of its reasoning.
d. Is the Court's decision unanimous? If any justices dissent, explain their reasoning.

17. GREGG V. GEORGIA
428 U.S. 153 (1976)

WHAT WAS THIS CASE ABOUT?

The story. Troy Leon Gregg was convicted in Georgia of two counts of armed robbery and two counts of murder. Evidence in Gregg's trial showed that on November 21, 1973, Gregg and a companion were hitchhiking north in Florida and were given a ride by two men. The bodies of the two men who offered the ride were found on November 22. Gregg admitted shooting and robbing the victims, although at first he claimed self-defense. Gregg was sentenced to death. Georgia's death penalty law provided for mandatory review by the Georgia Supreme Court, whose job it was to consider whether the death sentence imposed was influenced by "passion, prejudice, or any other arbitrary factor," whether the evidence supported the findings of one of ten "aggravated circumstances," and whether the penalty was "excessive or disproportionate" in relation to similar cases.

The Georgia Supreme Court reversed the sentencing for the robbery charge, holding that the death penalty was rarely imposed for armed robbery in Georgia. It upheld the sentence for the murders, however, holding that the sentencing did not result from any arbitrary factor and was not excessive or disproportionate to the penalty in similar cases. Gregg maintained that the death sentence he was given was "cruel and unusual punishment" and unconstitutional under the Eighth and 14th Amendments. The U.S. Supreme Court heard the case on March 31, 1976, and announced its decision regarding the case on July 2, 1976.

The question. Does the imposition of the death penalty for the crime of murder under Georgia law violate the Eighth and 14th Amendments?

The issues. At the heart of *Gregg v. Georgia* was the issue of whether the death penalty inflicts "cruel and unusual punishment" in violation of the Eighth Amendment and whether Gregg's civil rights as outlined in the 14th Amendment were being violated. Four years earlier, in *Furman v. Georgia,* the Supreme Court had nullified, or struck down, all death penalty statutes as they were then being applied in the United States. The issue in *Furman,* however, was that these state laws gave too much discretion to judges and juries in deciding whether to impose the death penalty.

In the wake of *Furman,* 35 states passed new laws. Some laws now made the death penalty a mandatory sentence for crimes such as killing a police officer. Other state laws adopted a bifurcated, or two-part, procedure in which the issue of guilt or innocence would be determined first, with a second hearing determining the penalty and whether the circumstances surrounding the crime justify the death sentence. On the same day that the Supreme Court decided *Gregg v. Georgia,* it ruled in *Woodson v. North Carolina* that mandatory death sentences were in violation of the Eighth Amendment. Gregg's fate, however, still revolved around the issue of whether the death penalty was cruel and unusual punishment. The Court focused on the two-stage approach to the death penalty and whether the state of Georgia had fairly applied this approach to Gregg and whether the Georgia statute prevents "arbitrary and disproportionate" death sentences. The Court also considered what constitutes "cruel and unusual punishment."

HOW WAS THE CASE DECIDED?

In an opinion written by Justice Potter Stewart, the Court ruled that the punishment of death for the crime of murder did not, invariably, violate the Eighth and 14th Amendments of the Constitution. In other words, when applied fairly, the death penalty is not unconstitutional.

WHAT DID THE COURT SAY ABOUT CONSTITUTIONAL RIGHTS?

According to the opinion delivered by Justice Stewart, the death penalty for persons convicted of first-degree murder is constitutional when it is proportionate to the severity of the crime. Georgia's law, the Court found, prevents arbitrary and disproportionate death sentences because of the following:

- The state's two-step procedure allows full consideration of the evidence. (First, guilt or innocence is determined and, in a second step, the sentence is determined.)
- The sentencing body must make specific factual findings to support the sentence.
- The mandatory review by the state Supreme Court ensures that the punishment is not disproportionate to the crime.

In reference to the phrase "cruel and unusual punishment," the Court noted that when the phrase was first written it referred to "barbarous" methods of punishment. In interpreting the Eighth Amendment today, "evolving standards of decency" must be acknowledged and the "punishment must not be excessive" or "inhumane" relative to these standards. According to Justice Stewart, "When a life has been taken deliberately . . . punishment by death is not . . . disproportionate to the crime." In the Court's opinion, an "extreme" crime is proportionate to an extreme penalty. In short, the Court's interpretation of the Constitution is that capital punishment is legal.

WHAT IMPLICATIONS DOES THIS CASE HAVE FOR THE FUTURE?

Since deciding *Gregg v. Georgia,* the Supreme Court has reviewed other cases that have given it the opportunity to reiterate its position that the death penalty itself is not unconstitutional but that it must be applied fairly. Of course, what is "fair," particularly to a person facing a death sentence, remains a source of controversy and debate. In *Thompson v. Oklahoma* (1988), the Court again considered the Eighth and 14th Amendments in deciding the issue. In *Thompson,* however, the Court decided that the death penalty was not justified— not because the death penalty itself is unconstitutional but because the sentence was not being applied fairly.

Today, the death penalty is illegal in some states but legal in many others. Hundreds of convicted felons await their execution on "death row." Assuredly, the Court will continue to decide cases that question the legality of capital punishment. Current arguments surrounding the death penalty include:

- Is it right for anyone to take the life of another, whether in an act of violence or as a punishment?
- Is the death penalty a deterrent to crime?
- What if it is found that the person put to death is innocent?

BRAIN TEASERS

1. Divide a sheet of paper into two columns labeled "For" and "Against." Under the appropriate heading, list arguments used for and against the death penalty.
2. Imagine that you are a Supreme Court justice hearing the case of *Gregg v. Georgia.* Write a paragraph either supporting or opposing the Court's ruling.
3. Do you think the death penalty is "cruel and unusual punishment"? Why or why not?

18. *REGENTS OF THE UNIVERSITY OF CALIFORNIA V. BAKKE*
438 U.S. 265 (1978)

WHAT WAS THIS CASE ABOUT?

The story. Allan Bakke wanted to become a doctor. Twice—in 1973 and again in 1974— he applied for admission to the medical school at the University of California at Davis. During these years the medical school operated two different admissions programs. Since the Civil Rights Act of 1964, there had been a lot of pressure from legislative and special interest groups for schools and other institutions to provide special admissions programs for minority students. There were, however, no specific guidelines on how this was to be accomplished.

In the medical school at the University of California at Davis, 84 of the 100 places in the incoming class were filled from the regular program, while 16 were set aside to be filled from the special program, which used a **quota system**. A quota is a share, or number, assigned for a particular purpose. The regular program was for students of all races, so long as they met admission requirements. One of these was a minimum grade point average. Only members of racial minorities could apply through the special program, however, and their college grade averages did not have to meet the minimum.

Bakke, a white male, applied through the regular program. His grades and test scores were good, and both years he got to the final stage of the admissions process. However, both years he was turned down. He thought he had been treated unfairly because in both years, students had been admitted through the special program whose grades and test scores were much lower than his own. He decided to sue the state university system, of which the University of California at Davis was a part. Bakke said the special program, established to fulfill the racial quota, had kept him from being admitted to medical school. He argued that the Davis admissions system violated his 14th Amendment right to equal protection of the law, and he asked the courts to order the medical school to admit him.

The California Supreme Court made two rulings. One said that the Davis admissions system was illegal and ordered that Bakke should be admitted to the medical school. The other ordered that in the future, race should not be given any consideration at all in admissions. Representatives of the California university system appealed both of these rulings to the United States Supreme Court.

The questions. First, does the use of a racial quota in admissions violate the equal protection clause of the 14th Amendment? Second, does the equal protection clause require that race be ignored completely? The United States Supreme Court had to consider these questions separately, because there might be ways of taking race into account that do not involve quotas.

The issues. Historically, most racial discrimination in our country has hurt members of racial minorities. Bakke complained about a different kind of discrimination. Sometimes called reverse discrimination, it hurt members of the racial majority, like Bakke, in order to help members of racial minorities. Since 1952 the Supreme Court had often spoken out against racial discrimination. Sometimes the famous words that Justice Harlan included in his dissent to *Plessy v. Ferguson* were quoted—that the Constitution is "color-blind." If the Constitution is "color-blind," then both forms of racial discrimination are unconstitutional—the traditional kind and the reverse kind. Before the *Bakke* case the Court had never had to consider reverse discrimination. Would it rule that both kinds of racial discrimination were unconstitutional?

Consider these facts as you think about the question. The main reason that the 14th Amendment was written was that African Americans who had recently been freed from slavery needed protection against discrimination by the white majority. This fact might lead you to think that the equal protection clause protects racial minorities more than the racial majority. On the other hand, what the amendment actually says is that no state may deny to *any* person the equal protection of the laws. This fact might lead you to think that the equal protection clause gives the same protection to people of all races. So the intent seems to have been to protect minorities while the wording does not specify this intent. As you can see, the Supreme Court was faced with a very difficult problem.

You may wonder what the 14th Amendment has to do with this case at all, because it speaks of what a state may do. Bakke's complaint was about a school. The reason that Bakke could use the 14th Amendment was that the school was part of a state-run university system.

HOW WAS THE CASE DECIDED?

The Court made a two-part ruling. One part agreed that the use of a racial quota in admissions to the medical school at the University of California at Davis was unconstitutional and ordered that Bakke should be admitted. The other part rejected the idea that an admissions system may never pay any attention to race at all.

WHAT DID THE COURT SAY ABOUT CONSTITUTIONAL RIGHTS?

Justice Lewis Powell wrote the Court's opinion. He said that the equal protection clause does not completely prohibit states from taking race into account when they are making laws and official policies but that it does make the consideration of race "suspect," or suspicious. When such a law or policy is challenged in court, judges must study it especially closely. The judges must apply a two-part test. First, are the purposes of the law or policy legitimate? Second, is the consideration given to race necessary to achieve these purposes? The law or policy is upheld only if the answer to both questions is yes.

California told the Court that its racial quota had four purposes. Let's see what Justice Powell said about each one.

Purpose 1. To correct the shortage of racial minorities in medical schools and among doctors.

Justice Powell said that this purpose was not acceptable. "Preferring members of any one group for no reason other than race or ethnic origin is discrimination for its own sake."

Purpose 2. To counteract the effects of racial discrimination in society.

Justice Powell said that this was an acceptable purpose. He approved of helping people who belong to groups that have been hurt by past racial discrimination. However, he said that helping them by hurting others is right only when it makes up for hurts that those specific others have done to them. There was no evidence that Allan Bakke or any other whites kept out of medical school by the quota had ever discriminated against people of racial minorities.

Purpose 3: To increase the number of doctors who will be willing to practice medicine in communities where there are not enough doctors now.

This purpose was also acceptable. But in order to bring more doctors to communities that needed them, was it necessary to have a racial quota in admissions to medical school? Justice Powell said that California had not shown this argument to be true.

Purpose 4: To improve education by making the student body more diverse.

This purpose, too, was acceptable. But Justice Powell made two points. First, racial diversity is only one aspect of overall diversity. Second, Justice Powell said that racial quotas are not needed to increase racial diversity. To prove this he discussed the experience of Harvard College. Harvard considers it a plus if an applicant belongs to a racial minority, but the college does not "insulate the individual from comparison with all other" applicants the way that a racial quota system would. In other words, the college compares all applicants equally. Yet the Harvard admissions system has been successful in increasing racial diversity in the Harvard student body.

WHAT IMPLICATIONS DOES THIS CASE HAVE FOR THE FUTURE?

You remember that one part of the Court's judgment agreed that the use of a racial quota in admissions to Davis Medical School was unconstitutional, while the other part rejected the idea that an admissions system may never pay any attention to race at all. What made this judgment unusual was that although a majority of five to four agreed with each part, Justice Powell was the only member of the Court to support both parts. The four who joined him in supporting the first part did not support the second part, and the four who did not agree with the first part joined him in supporting the second part. This situation shows how sharply the members of the Court disagree about reverse discrimination. Probably a majority will continue to hold that racial quotas and other forms of special treatment are unconstitutional. In a 1986 case called *Wygant v. Jackson Board of Education*, for instance, the Court said that members of racial minorities may not be given special treatment when a school board has to lay off some employees. However, disagreement about other ways in which government may take race into consideration in order to help members of racial minorities is likely to continue.

Justice Powell also stressed that the Court's decision in *Bakke* concerned only reverse racial discrimination. He warned that reverse sexual discrimination may or may not have to be treated the same way. So far, however, the Court has treated reverse discrimination pretty much the same whether it concerns race or sex. In a 1982 case called *Mississippi University for Women v. Hogan*, for example, the Court ruled that it was unconstitutional for a state-run school of nursing to refuse admission to men.

BRAIN TEASERS

1. Why did Allan Bakke sue the state university system of California? Why did he use the 14th Amendment in his argument to the courts?
2. Any policy that aims to give special help to members of groups that have been unfairly hurt by past discrimination is called an **affirmative action policy**. How would you set up affirmative action programs that do not involve quotas?

19. *PLYLER V. DOE*
457 U.S. 202 (1982)

WHAT WAS THIS CASE ABOUT?

The story. For a little more than 100 years the United States has had laws that limit immigration. Many of the people from other countries who apply to immigrate are accepted, but many others are not. Some people want to live here so much that they enter the country illegally. These people are officially called **undocumented aliens**, which means they are foreigners who do not have papers showing that they have permission to be in the country. Millions of undocumented aliens "now live in various states. Many work, pay taxes, and send their children to school, but they live in fear that they will be found out and sent back out of the country against their wills.

Texas is one of the states with an especially large number of undocumented aliens. In 1975 the Texas legislature passed a new education law. This law told local school districts that they would no longer receive any state money to educate the children of undocumented aliens. It also told the school districts that they could refuse to let the children of undocumented aliens enroll in public schools.

The Constitution promises due process of law not just to all citizens but to all people. Aliens can use our courts, even if they are here illegally. A lawsuit was started in Texas on behalf of several children of undocumented aliens. To conceal their identities, the true names of the children were not used, which is why the name Doe is used in the title of the case. Spokespeople for these children said that the new Texas law violated the 14th Amendment. They argued that when the Texas legislature ruled that the children could not receive the same education that other children received, it deprived them of equal protection of the laws. After winding through the lower courts, the case was decided by the United States Supreme Court in 1982.

The question. Does it violate the equal protection clause of the 14th Amendment for a state to deny public school enrollment to the children of undocumented aliens?

The issues. At first it may seem that the promise of "equal protection of the laws" means "every group of people must be treated exactly the same as every other." A moment's thought, however, will show you that the writers of the 14th Amendment could not have meant that. For example, people of different ages are not treated the same—only people eighteen years of age or older are allowed to vote. In fact, almost every law classifies people into groups that are treated differently. If there were something wrong with this, it is hard to see how there could be a system of laws at all. But classifications are more likely to be unfair than others. As you remember from *Regents of the University of California v. Bakke*, such classifications are called "suspect." Who decides which classifications are suspect and which are not? After careful study of the Constitution, it is the responsibility of the courts to decide the issue. The Texas law that was protested in *Plyler v. Doe* classified schoolchildren into two groups: (1) children of undocumented aliens and (2) all others. What the Supreme Court had to decide was whether this classification should be considered as suspect.

HOW WAS THE CASE DECIDED?

In an opinion written by Justice William Brennan, the Court ruled that the 14th

Amendment prohibits states from denying public school enrollment to the children of undocumented aliens. The vote was five to four.

WHAT DID THE COURT SAY ABOUT CONSTITUTIONAL RIGHTS?

Justice Brennan said in the ruling that education is not a constitutional right. He also said that grouping people into those who are in the country legally and those who are in the country illegally is not a suspect classification. These two statements may surprise you because they seem to lead to a different conclusion than the one Justice Brennan reached. What led him to his conclusion was what he said after making the two statements. Let's look at what he said after each one.

Although Justice Brennan said that education is not a constitutional right, he said that it is special in another way. Lack of education is an obstacle to achieving things by one's own merit. Justice Brennan thought that one of the purposes of the equal protection clause was to remove such obstacles.

Although Justice Brennan said that grouping people into those who are in the country legally and those who are in the country illegally was not a suspect classification, he said that applying the classification to children was hard to justify. Children cannot help it if they are in the country illegally; the parents brought the children into the country. Yet by keeping these children out of public school, Texas was punishing the children, not the parents.

Justice Brennan's conclusions was that the Texas law could be justified only if it was the only way to achieve some extremely important government goal. He could not think of any extremely important government goal for which the law was necessary, so he ruled against it.

WHAT IMPLICATIONS DOES THIS CASE HAVE FOR THE FUTURE?

The most obvious change resulting from the Court's decision is that children of undocumented aliens must be allowed to enroll in public schools. The way in which Justice Brennan reached this conclusion has implications for the future, too. This case was the first one in which the Court ever said that a government benefit that is not a constitutional

right can sometimes have constitutional protection anyway. Of course, the only government benefit the Court made this ruling about was education. It might, however, make this ruling about other government benefits that are special in the same way that education is. Remember that in Justice Brennan's view, what makes education special is that it removes obstacles to achieving things by one's own merit. There might be other government benefits that remove such obstacles, too.

Another possibility is that the Court will go in the other direction—not extending *Plyler v. Doe*, but reversing it. The vote in the case was very close—five to four. Since the case was decided there have been changes in the membership of the Court. These changes make it quite possible that the dissenter's views will become majority views on a similar case in the future.

What did the dissenting justices say? They firmly agreed that the Texas law was senseless. They said that it might bring about a society largely made up of **illiterate** people. They also admitted that Congress had failed to exercise leadership in solving United States immigration problems. These dissenters said that if it were up to them to make social policy, they would certainly make it differently. But then they stressed that it was not up to them to make social policy. Courts are not legislatures. The dissenters believed that for judges to say that something is unconstitutional when it is really only foolish is a violation of the separation of powers.

BRAIN TEASERS

1. Justice Brennan thought that one of the purposes of the equal protection clause was to remove obstacles to achieving things by one's own merit. Make a list of some other government benefits that remove such obstacles and explain your reasoning.

2. The Texas law classified schoolchildren into two groups: (1) children of undocumented aliens and (2) all others. In court Texas said that treating these two groups differently was necessary to achieve certain important government purposes. What important government purposes do you think Texas was trying to achieve?

3. The dissenting justices said that even though the Texas law was senseless, nothing in the Constitution could justify overruling it. Do you agree? Why or why not? Before you answer, examine the wording of the Constitution itself.

20. ROBERTS V. UNITED STATES JAYCEES
468 U.S. 69 (1984)

WHAT WAS THIS CASE ABOUT?

The story. The United States Jaycees (Junior Chamber of Commerce), founded as a young men's club in 1920, is a national organization with local chapters. Most members are business people. The local chapters help the members develop their management skills and other personal abilities. They also operate community charities and health programs and put on sporting events. Traditionally, the Jaycees limited regular membership to young men between the ages of 18 and 35. Women and older men could join, but only as associate members. Associate members paid lower dues than regular members, but they could not vote, hold office, or take part in some of the leadership training programs.

During the 1970s the Minneapolis and St. Paul chapters of the Jaycees began to allow women to become regular members. In 1978 the national organization tried to make them stop. It warned the chapters that they would lose their right to call themselves part of the Jaycees. After this warning the two chapters complained to the Minnesota Department of Human Rights. They said that the national Jaycees' rule against letting women be regular members violated a Minnesota human rights law. According to this law, businesses offering goods and services to the public may not discriminate on the basis of sex.

The national organization asked the federal courts for help. It said that by telling Jaycees who to let into their club, the state of Minnesota was violating the First Amendment. One federal court said this argument was incorrect. Then, a higher federal court said the argument was correct. In 1984 the case came to the United States Supreme Court for judgment.

The question. Is it a violation of the First Amendment for a state law to force the United States Jaycees to allow their local chapters to admit women as regular members?

The issues. The First Amendment says, "Congress shall make no law ... abridging ... the right of the people peaceably to assemble." Because of the 14th Amendment, this clause limits state legislatures in the same way that it limits Congress.

What exactly does it mean for the people to have a right "peaceably to assemble"? In its narrow meaning, the right protects democracy. Officials are not allowed to stop citizens from holding peaceful meetings to complain about what the government is doing. The Supreme Court, however, has said that the right has a broader meaning, too—"freedom of association."

The members of the national Jaycees organization thought that if some men and women wanted to be in a club together they should form their own club. They should not make an existing club change. To make an existing club change would interfere with its members' choices about whom to let into the club.

HOW WAS THE CASE DECIDED?

In an opinion written by Justice Brennan, the Court ruled that the Minnesota law did not violate the First Amendment promise of freedom of association. In other words, Minnesota could require the Jaycees chapters in the state to accept women as regular members instead of only as associate members.

WHAT DID THE COURT SAY ABOUT CONSTITUTIONAL RIGHTS?

Justice Brennan said that previous cases had shown that freedom of association has two different sides:

• Freedom of intimate association

The government cannot intrude on highly personal relationships.

• Freedom of expressive association

The government cannot stop people from assembling in order to exercise their other First Amendment rights, such as free speech and free exercise of religion.

To make his reasoning simpler Justice Brennan considered both sides of freedom of association in turn. First he asked whether or not the Minnesota law violated the Jaycees' freedom of intimate association. He said that it did not, because Jaycees chapters are very large and not particularly selective about who may join.

Next Justice Brennan asked if the Minnesota law violated the Jaycees' freedom of expressive association. He said that it did, because Jaycee members might have been brought together by shared opinions. Forcing them to accept new members they did not want might make it harder for them to express their opinions.

However, Justice Brennan said that violating the right to freedom of expressive association is not always wrong. A state law that violates the right is acceptable if the law meets three tests. First, the law must help achieve some important state purpose. Justice Brennan said it did—the purpose of fighting discrimination against women. Second, the purpose must not be to suppress opinions the state government does not like. Justice Brennan said that the law's purpose was not to suppress opinions. Third, the law must be the least restrictive of all possible ways to accomplish the purpose. Justice Brennan thought that it was.

After studying all three tests, Justice Brennan said that the Minnesota law did not violate the Jaycees' freedom of intimate association. It did violate the Jaycees' freedom of expressive association, but the violation was justified.

WHAT IMPLICATIONS DOES THIS CASE HAVE FOR THE FUTURE?

This case is very important for the future because it means that just calling a club "private" does not keep the government from making judgments about its membership policies. Notice, however, that the Court did not say that a private organization could not adopt a men-only policy. It only ruled on the Jaycees. The fact that Jaycee chapters are large and open to most people was very influential. If the Court were asked to rule on a private organization that was more intimate than the Jaycees, it might rule differently.

Remember, too, that only one of the Jaycees' membership policies was challenged in this case. The rule that regular members must be men was overturned, but the rule that regular members must be between 18 and 35 years of age is still in force. We don't know how the Court might have dealt with a challenge to the age rule.

BRAIN TEASERS

Pretend that a state called New Fangle lies just between New York and New Jersey. The New Fangle state legislature passes a law against all forms of age and sex discrimination. The state's Anti-Discrimination Commission immediately files criminal charges against the following groups:

a. a religious denomination because it accepts only men as ministers

b. a feminist organization because it accepts only women as members

c. a community service club because it accepts only people under 18 years of age as members

d. a neighborhood social club because it accepts only people between the ages of 40 and 55 as members

Each group appeals to the federal courts that its First Amendment right to freedom of association has been violated. Eventually all four cases reach the United States Supreme Court. Imagine that you are a justice on the Supreme Court. Choose any two of these cases. For each one that you choose, write a Supreme Court opinion telling how the case should be settled and why. You must consider every one of the arguments you've read about in this lesson, but you are free to agree or disagree with the arguments. Make your opinion as realistic as you can.

21. CENTRAL HUDSON GAS & ELECTRIC CORPORATION V. PUBLIC SERVICE COMMISSION
447 U.S. 557 (1980)

WHAT WAS THIS CASE ABOUT?

The story. In the state of New York electric utility companies are regulated by the Public

Service Commission. Late in 1973 the Commission decided that there was an energy shortage. There was not enough fuel available to make all the electricity that consumers might want during the coming winter. One of the steps the Commission took to deal with this crisis was to tell electric utility companies that they were no longer allowed to make advertisements urging people to use electricity or buy electrical products. This kind of advertising is called promotional advertising because it promotes a product.

Three years later, even though there was plenty of fuel, the Commission decided to continue the promotional-advertising ban. The Commission's reasoning was that promotional advertising works against the national policy of conserving energy. Central Hudson Gas & Electric Corporation opposed this decision. It asked the courts for help, saying that the ban on promotional advertising violated the First Amendment promise of freedom of speech. In 1980 the case reached the United States Supreme Court.

The question. Does a state ban on promotional advertising by an electric utility violate the First Amendment promise of free speech? Again the case involved the 14th Amendment because it allows the First Amendment to be applied to a state.

The issues. Central Hudson Gas & Electric Corporation said that advertising should be allowed because it was commercial speech. The New York Public Service Commission disagreed. In earlier cases the Court had defined commercial speech as speech that does nothing more than propose that somebody buy something. The Court had also said that commercial speech had some constitutional protection but not as much as some other kinds of speech. This definition was rather mysterious. How much protection did commercial speech have? Did it have so much protection that promotional advertising could not be banned?

HOW WAS THE CASE DECIDED?

In an opinion written by Justice Lewis Powell, the Court ruled that the New York Public Service Commission's ban on promotional advertising for electricity violated the First Amendment.

WHAT DID THE COURT SAY ABOUT CONSTITUTIONAL RIGHTS?

The core of Justice Powell's opinion was a rule for deciding which kinds of restrictions on commercial speech are acceptable. This rule said that whenever a restriction on commercial speech is challenged in court, judges must test it in four ways:

- To what kind of commercial speech does the restriction apply? Is it the kind that the First Amendment might protect?

There is no need to go on to the other three tests unless the answer to the second part of this test is yes. An advertisement has First Amendment protection only if it is not misleading and does not invite people to do things that are against the law.

- Does the government have a "substantial interest" in restricting this kind of speech?

This test means that the government must have a fairly important purpose in mind when it draws up the restriction.

- Does the restriction "directly advance" this interest?

This test means that it is not enough for the government to *think* that the restriction helps to achieve its purpose. The restriction *must* help to achieve the purpose and the help must be direct.

- Could a less extensive restriction serve this interest just as well?

The government should not interfere with commercial speech any more than it has to. If a less extensive restriction would achieve its purpose just as well as a more extensive restriction, then the more extensive restriction should not be used.

Next, Justice Powell applied the four tests to the New York Public Service Commission's ban on promotional advertising. In this case the most important test turned out to be the last. Justice Powell agreed with Central Hudson that the Constitution gives promotional advertising for electricity and electrical products some protection. Then he agreed with the Commission that the government does have a substantial interest in energy matters. It also agreed that the ban on such advertising helped achieve a fairly important government purpose—conservation of energy. He said, however, that a partial ban could have conserved energy just as well as a complete ban. A partial ban might even have worked better. Some ways of using electricity are more efficient than other ways, and some electrical products are more efficient than other products. Advertising that promoted these ways and these products might actually save energy rather than waste it. Because the ban was broader than it needed to be, it was unconstitutional.

WHAT IMPLICATIONS DOES THIS CASE HAVE FOR THE FUTURE?

The most important thing to come from this case is a legal test for deciding which regulations on commercial speech are constitutional and which are not. Notice, however, that the legal test is very complicated and must be applied on a case-by-case basis. Thus, the way the test is applied will still depend a great deal on the judgment of the individual justices. In general, the more a legal rule depends on the judgment of the individual justices, the less sure people are about which regulations the Court will approve and which they will disapprove. In turn, the less sure people are, the more willing they are to take a chance on challenging regulations they dislike. Thus, we can expect that there will be more commercial speech cases in the future. If there are many commercial speech cases, the justices may grow weary of them. Then the Court will probably try to come up with another legal test that is easier to apply.

BRAIN TEASERS

1. Suppose you are a member of Congress and want to pass a law limiting promotional advertising for cigarettes—perhaps a total ban, perhaps a partial ban. Certainly the tobacco companies would challenge such a law. Think carefully about all four parts of Justice Powell's test. How should you explain the law's purposes and how extensive should you make it in order to make sure that it will survive challenge in the federal court?

2. Suppose you are the president of a tobacco company. You want as few restrictions on promotional advertising for cigarettes as possible. You know about congressional efforts to limit promotional advertising for cigarettes, and you are anxious about these efforts. Think about all four parts of Justice Powell's test. What kind of explanation of the law's purposes do you hope Congress will give, and how extensive do you hope Congress will make the law so that it will *not* survive challenge in the federal courts?

22. *HAZELWOOD SCHOOL DISTRICT V. KUHLMEIER*
484 U.S. 260 (1988)

WHAT WAS THIS CASE ABOUT?

The story. Hazelwood East High School is in St. Louis County, Missouri. Every three weeks the Journalism II class published a paper called *Spectrum*. The paper was distributed to more than 4,500 students, school workers, and members of the community. Because *Spectrum* was sponsored by the school, the articles that the journalism class proposed for each edition were submitted to the school administration for approval.

On May 10, 1983, the principal of the high school objected to two articles scheduled to appear in *Spectrum's* May 13 edition. There was no time to change the articles, so the principal instructed the journalism teacher to leave the two articles out of the school newspaper. He also informed school district officials of his decision, and they agreed that he had done the right thing. One of the articles was about pregnant students at Hazelwood East. Although it did not use the students' real names, the principal feared that readers might be able to tell who the students were from the other information in the article. He was also concerned about some of the article's references to other controversial issues. He thought that the issues discussed were all right for most students to read but might be inappropriate for some of the younger students.

The other article was about how Hazelwood East students were affected by their parents' divorces. It included one student's very personal complaints about her divorced father and mother. What worried the principal was that the student was identified by name. Because of this, he thought that the student's parents should have been given a chance to respond or to give their permission for the remarks to be published.

The journalism teacher, Howard Emerson, withheld the two articles from publication just as he had been instructed. Three students on the newspaper staff said that their First Amendment rights to freedom of speech were being violated. They sued the principal, Howard Emerson, various other officials, and the school district as a whole. After slowly working its way through the lower courts, the case was finally settled by the United States Supreme Court in 1988.

The question. Is it a violation of the First Amendment for high school authorities to exercise editorial control over the content of a school-sponsored newspaper produced in a journalism class?

The issues. You remember from *Tinker v. Des Moines Independent Community School District* that students do not "shed their constitutional rights to freedom of speech or expression at the schoolhouse gate." The Court did say in *Tinker*, however, that student action that resembles speech could be punished if it disrupted the educational process. That rule could have been applied in *Kuhlmeier*, too. The Court decided not to apply it. Why? Had the Court changed its mind?

No. The Court still agreed with what it had said in *Tinker*. But it decided that the issues in *Tinker* and in *Kuhlmeier* were different. *Tinker*, it said, was about whether or not a school could punish students for expressing their opinions. *Kuhlmeier*, by contrast, was about whether a school had to *help* students express their opinions. The Court thought that it would be a mistake to try to treat these two issues as though they were the same. But why does the issue of helping students express their opinions come up in *Kuhlmeier*? Because the students in the case wanted to express their opinions in a school-sponsored newspaper produced in their journalism class.

HOW WAS THE CASE DECIDED?

In an opinion written by Justice Byron White, the Court ruled that the First Amendment rights of the students who wrote *Spectrum* had not been violated when the school principal withheld their articles from publication.

WHAT DID THE COURTS SAY ABOUT CONSTITUTIONAL RIGHTS?

Justice White made extensive use of principles the Court had developed in cases that arose after *Tinker*. You remember that one of the issues not settled in *Tinker* was if teenagers have the same speech rights as adults. The Court had settled this issue in another case. It had announced that speech rights of teenagers "are not automatically coextensive with [do not extend as far as] the rights of adults in other settings." These rights must be "applied in light of the special characteristics of the school environment," and the school need not permit speech that clashes with its "basic educational mission." What this meant in *Kuhlmeier* was that the speech rights of the students who worked on *Spectrum* were not necessarily as far-reaching as the speech rights of adults working on a regular newspaper.

What about the idea that Hazelwood East High School should have helped the students on the *Spectrum* staff express the opinions that the cancelled articles contained? Justice White agreed that sometimes officials should actually help free speech along instead of just allowing it. But he said that this kind of help is only required in "public forums"—places such as streets and parks, which in the past "have been used for purposes of assembly, communicating thoughts between citizens, and discussing public questions." So he asked, "Was *Spectrum* a public forum?" He said that two facts showed that it was not. First, working on *Spectrum* was available only to students in the journalism class. Working on the newspaper was not available to the general public or even to all students. Second, *Spectrum* was reserved for a special purpose. Its only reason for existence was to teach students journalism. What this meant for *Kuhlmeier* was that the school did not have to help the students on the *Spectrum* staff express their opinions except in ways that helped teach them journalism.

Finally, Justice White listed a number of different reasons that a school might exercise editorial control as a publisher of a school newspaper. Some of these reasons were taken from other cases and some were new. A school does not have to publish articles in any of the following cases:

- when they would "substantially interfere with its work"
- when they would "impinge upon the rights of other students"
- when they are "ungrammatical" or "poorly written"
- when they are "inadequately researched"
- when they are "biased" or "profane"
- when they are "unsuitable for immature audiences"

Justice White said that if schools could not refuse to publish articles of these kinds, they would not be able to awaken students to the values that are important to our culture, prepare students for later professional training, or help them adjust normally to their environment.

WHAT IMPLICATIONS DOES THIS CASE HAVE FOR THE FUTURE?

In order to help judges decide future cases, Justice White summed up his conclusions in a rule. We can paraphrase this rule in question-and-answer style as follows:

- Can educators, acting as editors, limit what students say in school newspapers?
  Yes, but only if they can justify the limitations in a certain way.

- In what was must the limitations be justified?
  There must be a good reason to think that the limitations they want to impose will promote the educational purposes of the school.
- What kinds of limitations are acceptable?
  They may limit both what the students say and how they say it.
- Do the same rules apply to student speech in all other settings?
  No, but they do apply to student speech in some other settings.
- To what other settings do they apply?
  To all student speech in school-sponsored speech activities.

BRAIN TEASERS

1. The rule that Justice White developed in *Kuhlmeier* applies not to all student speech but only to student speech in school-sponsored speech activities. Divide a sheet of paper into two columns. In one column give examples of student speech that occurs in school-sponsored speech activities. In the other column give examples of student speech that occurs in school but not in school-sponsored speech activities.
2. Explain the differences between the rules applied in *Tinker* and in *Kuhlmeier.* Why did Justice White refuse to apply the *Tinker* rule to the *Kuhlmeier* situation?
3. Do you think that the outcome in *Kuhlmeier* would have been different if the *Tinker* principle had been applied? Why or why not? Explain your answer.

23. *TEXAS V. JOHNSON*
491 U.S. 397 (1989)

WHAT WAS THIS CASE ABOUT?

The story. Heated political protests and demonstrations, reminiscent of the widespread antiwar protests of the 1960s and 70s, ensued during the 1984 Republican National Convention held in Dallas, Texas. Many of the protesters were voicing their opposition to the policies of the administration of President Ronald Reagan. Outside Dallas City Hall, where some of the demonstrators had gathered, Gregory Lee Johnson doused a U.S. flag with kerosene and set it on fire as a means of political protest.

Johnson was arrested and charged with the desecration of a venerated object—a Texas law made it a crime to desecrate a state or national flag. Johnson was convicted and sentenced to one year in prison and fined $2,000. The Texas Court of Criminal Appeals, however, reversed the conviction, maintaining that Johnson's burning of the flag was actually a form of symbolic speech and, therefore, protected by the First Amendment. The state of Texas then appealed to the U.S. Supreme Court. Oral arguments were presented in March 1989. The Court announced its decision on June 21.

The question. Does the First Amendment protect the desecration of the U.S. flag as a form of symbolic speech?

The issues. The First Amendment states, in part, that "Congress shall make no law . . . abridging the freedom of speech." What actions, however, can be included under the term *speech*? According to the Texas Court of Criminal Appeals, which overturned Johnson's conviction, burning a flag falls under this protected term. The Texas Court stated, "Given the context of an organized demonstration, speeches, slogans, and the distribution of literature, anyone who observed . . . would have understood the message. . . . The act for which [Johnson] was convicted was clearly 'speech' contemplated by the First Amendment. . . ." The state of Texas, however, argued that its interest was in preserving the flag as a symbol of national unity and in preventing breaches of the peace. It was now up to the Supreme Court to decide the validity of Johnson's conviction.

HOW WAS THE CASE DECIDED?

In an opinion written by Justice William Brennan, the Supreme Court ruled that Johnson's conviction was inconsistent with the First Amendment. In other words, Johnson was within his constitutional rights when he burned the U.S. flag in protest. The Court's vote was five to four.

WHAT DID THE COURT SAY ABOUT CONSTITUTIONAL RIGHTS?

You have read about a similar case, *Tinker v. Des Moines Independent Community School District* (1969), in which the Supreme Court considered the First Amendment's promise of freedom of speech. In *Texas v. Johnson,* Justice Brennan concluded that Johnson's act was "expressive conduct" in that he was attempting to "convey a . . . message." Thus, his burning of the flag as a form of symbolic speech—like the students wearing armbands in Des Moines in their political protest—is protected by the First Amendment. According to Brennan, "Government may not prohibit the expression of an idea simply because society finds the idea itself offensive."

Citing the state of Texas' interest in preventing breaches of the peace and preserving the flag as a symbol of national unity, Justice Brennan stated that Johnson's expression posed no threat to the peace and that the burning of the flag did not endanger the flag's status as a national symbol. As a result, the Texas statute prohibiting the desecration of a venerated object was declared unconstitutional and invalid.

WHAT IMPLICATIONS DOES THIS CASE HAVE FOR THE FUTURE?

As in *Tinker,* critics of the Court's ruling in *Texas v. Johnson* argued that the Court had interpreted the term *speech* too broadly. Since *Texas v. Johnson,* the Supreme Court has had other opportunities to reiterate its position that symbolic speech, or "nonverbal expression," is indeed protected by the First Amendment. In direct response to the Court's controversial ruling in *Texas,* the U.S. Congress passed the Flag Protection Act of 1989. The Supreme Court ruled this act unconstitutional in *The United States v. Eichman* (496 U.S. 310) in June 1990.

BRAIN TEASERS

1. Think of another form of "symbolic speech" that could be argued as being protected by the First Amendment. Write a brief debate expressing two opposing views.
2. Despite the opinion of the Court, do you think a person has a right to desecrate the U.S. flag as a form of protest? Why or why not?
3. In your own words, explain what Justice Brennan meant when he wrote that "We do not consecrate the flag by punishing its desecration, for in doing so we dilute the freedom that this cherished emblem represents."

24. BOARD OF EDUCATION OF THE WESTSIDE COMMUNITY SCHOOLS V. MERGENS
496 U.S. 226 (1990)

WHAT WAS THIS CASE ABOUT?

The story. When Bridget Mergens approached Westside High School's principal in January 1985 and asked that a Bible study group be allowed to meet after school, her request was denied. Westside's associate superintendent and its superintendent agreed with the principal's decision. Mergens appealed to the Board of Education, which also denied her request. Then a senior in the Omaha, Nebraska, high school, the 18-year-old Mergens was shocked and angry. Westside school officials cited the establishment clause of the First Amendment and the separation of church and state as the basis for its refusal to allow the Bible study group to meet at the school. Believing that her rights were being violated, the teenager set out to appeal the decision by taking legal action against the school district.

In her suit, Mergens claimed that the school district's refusal to allow a Christian club to meet at the school violated the 1984 Equal Access Act. The act forbids public secondary schools that receive federal funds and that maintain a "limited open forum" from denying "equal access" to extracurricular groups that wish to meet within that forum on the basis of the "religious, political, philosophical, or other content of the speech" at such meetings. In other words, if a public school allows one extracurricular group to meet at the school, it must allow others to meet. It cannot forbid a group from meeting even if the group is religion-oriented. Westside Community Schools countered that the Equal Access Act violated the establishment clause. The U.S. District Court for Nebraska agreed with Westside Schools, holding that the act did not apply because Westside High School did not have a "limited open forum" because all of the school's clubs were curriculum-related. The Eighth Circuit Court of Appeals, however, reversed the decision, saying that the Circuit Court was wrong in concluding that all of Westside's student clubs were curriculum-related and that the school did indeed maintain a "limited open forum." It also rejected Westside Schools' argument that the Equal Access Act violated the establishment clause of the First Amendment. The U.S. Supreme Court agreed to review the case.

The questions. Can public secondary schools deny equal access to voluntary religious clubs? Does the Equal Access Act violate the establishment clause of the First Amendment?

The issues. Over the years and amid much controversy, the Supreme Court has consistently ruled against school-sponsored prayer and other religious activities. As early as

1947, in *Everson v. Board of Education of Ewing Township,* the Court held that the establishment clause of the First Amendment requires a "wall of separation" between church and state. From the perspective of Westside Schools, a religious club meeting at the high school would be tearing down this wall.

As you know, the First Amendment forbids the government from setting up or providing for an established church. The First Amendment has also been interpreted to forbid the government from endorsing or aiding any religious doctrine. But how does the amendment apply to public schools and extracurricular activities? If other student groups can meet after school on school grounds, why is a student Bible study group prevented from doing so? To understand the arguments presented in the case, it is important to first explore the meanings of several key phrases. Was the proposed Bible study group a "noncurriculum student group," and, if so, is it entitled to "equal access"? What is a "limited open forum" as used in the Equal Access Act? In denying the religious group equal access, was the school district doing so on the basis of the group's "religious" content? The Supreme Court considered these issues and more.

HOW WAS THE CASE DECIDED?

In an opinion written by Justice Sandra Day O'Connor, the Court ruled on June 4, 1990, that the 1984 Equal Access Act does not violate the establishment clause of the First Amendment. Student religious groups, therefore, must be given the same access to public secondary schools as other noncurriculum groups.

WHAT DID THE COURT SAY ABOUT CONSTITUTIONAL RIGHTS?

In its ruling, the Court held that the term "noncurriculum student group" can be interpreted to mean any student group that is unrelated to the courses offered by the school. If the focus of the group meetings relates to subject matter taught at the school in an actual course, then the group is "curriculum related." If the school allows other noncurriculum-related groups to meet at the school, then the school maintains a "limited open forum." According to the ruling, this kind of forum requires the school to allow equal access to all extracurricular groups.

The Court also held that applying the Equal Access Act here does not "endorse" or "advance" religion and, therefore, is not in violation of the Constitution. In other words, in providing a place for the Bible study group to meet, the high school was not supporting any particular religious view or practice. According to the Court, the Equal Access Act's requirement that student religious groups be given the same access to schools as other non-curriculum-related groups does not risk "excessive entanglement between government and religion." By denying the religious club equal access to the school, Westside was in violation of the Equal Access Act.

WHAT IMPLICATIONS DOES THIS CASE HAVE FOR THE FUTURE?

In his dissent in *Mergens,* Justice John Paul Stevens said, "Can Congress really have intended to issue an order to every public high school . . . that if you sponsor a chess club, a scuba diving club, or a French club—without having formal classes in those subjects—you must also open your doors to every religious, political, or social organization, no matter how controversial or distasteful its views may be? I think not." In the wake of *Mergens,* many school officials voiced similar views.

A public school that absolutely does not want an extracurricular religious group to meet on school premises—regardless of the group's legal right to do so—has at least two options. It can forgo all government funding, which would remove its status as a "public school." Or, it can abolish all of its extracurricular groups, which would mean that the school no longer maintained a "limited open forum." It is doubtful whether any public school would choose either option.

BRAIN TEASERS

1. Your school does not offer a course that teaches the game of chess. A group of students wishes to form a chess club that will meet on school grounds after regular school hours. There are other extracurricular clubs that meet at your school. Does the proposed chess club fall under the protective guidelines of the 1984 Equal Access Act? Why or why not?

2. Review the comment made by Justice Stevens in his dissent. Do you agree or disagree with Justice Stevens? If you were a Supreme Court justice hearing *Mergens,* how would you have voted?

3. How did the Supreme Court address the issue of separation between church and state in this case?

25. *BOARD OF EDUCATION OF KIRYAS JOEL VILLAGE SCHOOL DISTRICT V. GRUMET*
114 U.S. 2481 (1994)

WHAT WAS THIS CASE ABOUT?

The story. New York's Village of Kiryas Joel is home to more than 10,000 members of the Satmar Hasidic religious sect, a strict form of Judaism. The Satmars have been compared to the Amish in that they shun most modern conveniences and wear distinctive clothing. The Satmars employ strict interpretations of the Torah, speak Yiddish as their first language, and have special dietary restrictions. To escape religious persecution, the Satmars migrated during this century from the Romanian border town of Satu Mare, from which the group's name originates.

Once an undeveloped subdivision of Monroe, New York, Kiryas Joel was incorporated as a self-governing village in 1977. When it seceded from Monroe, Kiryas Joel's boundaries were drawn to include only Satmar families. The village's children attended private religious schools. Because these schools could not adequately accommodate Kiryas Joel's more than 100 children with disabilities, in 1989 the state created a public-school district specifically for these children. Citing the First Amendment, Louis Grumet, then president of the New York Association of School Boards, challenged the legality of a state-funded district created to serve the children of a religious group. The state of New York ruled against the Kiryas Joel School District. The Supreme Court heard the case in March 1994.

The question. Did the New York state legislature act constitutionally when it established a state-funded school district for the children with disabilities of the Village of Kiryas Joel, a religious enclave?

The issues. This was not the first time that the fate of Kiryas Joel's children with disabilities was in the hands of the Supreme Court. The Monroe-Woodbury Central School District's attempt to provide special services to these children was discontinued after the Court's ruling in *Aguilar v. Felton* (1985) declared that public-school teachers could not be sent into private religious schools. After *Aguilar,* some Satmar families tried sending their children to Monroe's nearby public schools, but the children were "traumatized" by ridicule from non-Satmar children. When the families then claimed that their children were legally entitled to special programs currently unavailable, the state created a special school district for the Village of Kiryas Joel.

The key issues in *Kiryas Joel v. Grumet* were the children's entitlement to receive needed special programs, the First Amendment's establishment clause, which calls for the separation of church and state, and the role of the state in accommodating religion to "alleviate special burdens."

HOW WAS THE CASE DECIDED?

In an opinion written by Justice David Souter, the Supreme Court ruled that in creating a special school district for a religious enclave incorporated as a village to exclude all but its practitioners, New York violated the establishment clause of the First Amendment.

WHAT DID THE COURT SAY ABOUT CONSTITUTIONAL RIGHTS?

Justice Souter wrote that "The Constitution allows the state to accommodate religious needs by alleviating special burdens. . . ." This, however, "is not a principle without limits . . . Neutrality among religions must be honored." Justice Souter's argument against Kiryas Joel centered on the establishment clause of the First Amendment, which ensures that a state act with neutrality toward religion. In other words, a state cannot favor "one religion over another" or "religion to irreligion." There was no way of knowing whether another group in a similar situation would be granted the same privilege as Kiryas Joel. In addition, according to the Court, the Village of Kiryas Joel had

other alternatives to pursue to alleviate its "burden." For example, the Monroe-Woodbury Central School District could legally offer an appropriate program at a "neutral" site to serve the children with disabilities.

Justice Kennedy noted a "fine line between the voluntary association that leads to a political community comprised of people who share a common religious faith, and the forced separation that occurs when the government draws explicit political boundaries on the basis of peoples' faith."

WHAT IMPLICATIONS DOES THIS CASE HAVE FOR THE FUTURE?

While the government cannot "endorse" or "advance" religion, it must also protect the rights of all, regardless of religion. Some people believe that the Supreme Court contradicts itself in its efforts to abide by these tenets. In his dissent, Justice Antonin Scalia echoed that criticism: "The Founding Fathers would be astonished to find that the Establishment Clause—which they designed 'to insure that no one powerful sect . . . could use political or governmental power to punish dissenters'— has been employed to prohibit . . . American accommodation of the religious practices . . . of a tiny minority sect. . . . Once this Court has abandoned text and history as guides, nothing prevents it from calling religious toleration the establishment of religion." The case of *Kiryas Joel* made it clear that a religious group cannot be granted its own government-funded school district. What will continue to be debated is whether the government's obligation to protect the rights of all is counter to the Court's ruling.

BRAIN TEASERS

1. Do you think the state of New York erred in setting up a public-school district for the children with disabilities of the Village of Kiryas Joel? Why or why not?
2. Explain how this Supreme Court case relates to the constitutional concept of separation of church and state.
3. Do you think there is truth in Justice Scalia's dissenting argument that the Court could someday call "religious toleration the establishment of religion"? Explain your answer.

26. MADSEN V. WOMEN'S HEALTH CENTER, INC.
114 U.S. 2516 (1994)

WHAT WAS THIS CASE ABOUT?

The story. In September 1992, after antiabortion protesters continued to picket and demonstrate outside the Women's Health Center, a Melbourne, Florida, abortion clinic, a Florida state court issued an injunction to prevent the protesters from blocking or interfering with public access to the facility and from abusing persons leaving or entering the clinic. Six months later, when protesters continued to impede access to the clinic, distribute antiabortion literature, chant using bullhorns and loudspeakers, and harass clinic workers at their homes, the clinic's operators sought to broaden the injunction. A doctor testified that the protesters' actions endangered the health of patients by causing added stress or by causing patients to delay clinic appointments.

The Florida Circuit Court amended the injunction, creating a 36-foot buffer zone around the clinic's entrances and driveway and around private property to the north and west of the building. It placed restrictions on excessive noise and the use of "observable images," such as offensive photographs. It also created a 300-foot buffer zone around clinic workers' residences.

The protesters claimed that the amended injunction violated their First Amendment right to freedom of speech. The Florida Supreme Court upheld the Circuit Court's decision. Before the state's Supreme Court decision was announced, however, the Florida Court of Appeals heard a separate challenge to the same injunction. The Appeals Court struck down the injunction, ruling that the concerns for public safety and order were protected under already established laws and that there was no need to infringe upon the First Amendment rights of others. To resolve the dispute between the Florida Supreme Court and the state's Court of Appeals regarding the constitutionality of the Circuit Court's amended injunction, the U.S. Supreme Court agreed to hear the case.

The question. Did a Florida Circuit Court's amended injunction against antiabortion protesters outside a central Florida abortion clinic violate the protesters' First Amendment right of freedom of speech?

The issues. In resolving the dispute the U.S. Supreme Court had to examine the arguments presented by both courts. For example, in upholding the amended injunction, the Florida Supreme Court had found it to be a "content neutral" restriction on free speech rather than the "content-based" restriction asserted by the Court of Appeals. According to the Florida Supreme Court, the restrictions were not directed at the protesters' antiabortion message but at their actions. The U.S. Supreme Court also had to determine whether the injunction "burdens no more speech than necessary to serve a government interest." The Court analyzed each provision of the amended injunction to determine its constitutionality.

HOW WAS THE CASE DECIDED?

In an opinion written by Chief Justice William Rehnquist, the Supreme Court ruled that the establishment of a 36-foot buffer zone from which demonstrators are excluded "passes muster under the First Amendment, but several other provisions of the injunction do not." In other words, the Court upheld parts of the amended injunction and struck down other parts.

WHAT DID THE COURT SAY ABOUT CONSTITUTIONAL RIGHTS?

In its decision, the U.S. Supreme Court:

- upheld the 36-foot buffer zone around the clinic's entrances and driveway, ruling that it did not burden more speech than necessary to protect access to the clinic, but struck down the buffer zone around the private property to the clinic's north and west;
- upheld the injunction's noise restrictions, noting that "The First Amendment does not demand that patients undertake Herculean efforts to escape the cacophony of political protests";
- struck down the ban on "images observable" as an unreasonable restriction, pointing out that the clinic could "pull its curtains";
- struck down a 300-foot buffer zone around staff residences, ruling that it "sweep[s] more broadly than necessary."

The Court agreed with the Florida Supreme Court that the injunction was "content neutral," ruling that "none of the restrictions imposed by the court were directed at the . . . message." In short, the Court's majority opinion stated that while antiabortion protesters have a right to free speech, that right cannot infringe upon the well-being of others and, in the context of the injunction, must be limited. According to the Court, "The combination of the governmental interests identified by the Florida Supreme Court—protecting a pregnant woman's freedom to seek lawful medical or counseling services, ensuring public safety and order, promoting the free flow of traffic, . . . protecting . . . property rights, and assuring residential privacy—is quite sufficient to justify an appropriately tailored injunction."

WHAT IMPLICATIONS DOES THIS CASE HAVE FOR THE FUTURE?

In striking down the amended injunction, the Florida Appeals Court called the dispute "a clash between an actual prohibition of speech and a potential hindrance to the free exercise of abortion rights." The Supreme Court's 1973 ruling in *Roe v. Wade* gave women the legal right to abortion. The questions to consider relative to cases like *Madsen* include: Is a woman's right to an abortion impeded by protesters who block entrances to abortion clinics, harass physicians and other medical personnel, and threaten the health of women by causing added stress? Do such actions not interfere with a woman's constitutional right to privacy expressly mentioned in *Roe v. Wade?* As you have learned, efforts to overturn the Court's decision in *Roe v. Wade* are ongoing. These efforts likely will result in more cases like *Madsen.*

BRAIN TEASERS

1. Write two brief paragraphs. In one paragraph, express the view of a doctor working at the clinic. In another, express the view of an antiabortion protester who supports demonstrations near entrances to abortion clinics.
2. The Court found that the injunction was "content neutral." In other words, the injunction did not attack the antiabortion message voiced by the protesters but the methods used to voice the message. Do you agree with this finding?

Magna Carta [1215]

John, by the grace of God, king of England, lord of Ireland, duke of Normandy and Aquitaine, and count of Anjou, to the archbishops, bishops, abbots, earls, barons, justiciars, foresters, sheriffs, stewards, servants, and to all his bailiffs and faithful subjects, greeting. Know that we, out of reverence for God and for the salvation of our soul and those of all our ancestors and heirs, for the honour of God and the exaltation of holy church, and for the reform of our realm, on the advice of our venerable fathers, Stephen, archbishop of Canterbury, primate of all England and cardinal of the holy Roman church, Henry archbishop of Dublin, William of London, Peter of Winchester, Jocelyn of Bath and Glastonbury, Hugh of Lincoln, Walter of Worcester, William of Coventry and Benedict of Rochester, bishops, of master Pandulf, subdeacon and member of the household of the lord pope, of brother Aymeric, master of the order of Knights Templar in England, and of the noble men William Marshal earl of Pembroke, William earl of Salisbury, William earl of Warenne, William earl of Arundel, Alan of Galloway constable of Scotland, Warin fitz Gerold, Peter fitz Herbert, Hubert de Burgh seneschal of Poitou, Hugh de Neville, Matthew fitz Herbert, Thomas Basset, Alan Basset, Philip de Aubeney, Robert of Ropsley, John Marshal, John fitz Hugh, and others, our faithful subjects:

[1] In the first place have granted to God, and by this our present charter confirmed for us and our heirs for ever that the English church shall be free, and shall have its rights undiminished and its liberties unimpaired; and it is our will that it be thus observed; which is evident from the fact that before the quarrel between us and our barons began, we willingly and spontaneously granted and by our charter confirmed the freedom of elections which is reckoned most important and very essential to the English church, and obtained confirmation of it from the lord pope Innocent III; the which we will observe and we wish our heirs to observe it in good faith for ever. We have also granted to all free men of our kingdom, for ourselves and our heirs for ever, all the liberties written below, to be had and held by them and their heirs of us and our heirs.

[2] If any of our earls or barons or others holding of us in chief by knight service dies, and at his death his hear be of full age and owe relief he shall have his inheritance on payment of the old relief, namely the heir or heirs of an earl £100 for a whole earl's barony, the heir or heirs of a baron £100 for a whole barony, the heir or heirs of a knight 100s, at most, for a whole knight's fee; and he who owes less shall give less according to the ancient usage of fiefs.

[3] If, however, the heir of any such be under age and a ward, he shall have his inheritance when he comes of age without paying relief and without making fine.

[4] The guardian of the land of such an heir who is under age shall take from the land of the heir no more than reasonable revenues, reasonable customary dues and reasonable services and that without destruction and waste of men or goods; and if we commit the wardship of the land of any such to a sheriff, or to any other who is answerable to us for its revenues, and he destroys or wastes what he has wardship of, we will take compensation from him and the land shall be committed to two lawful and discreet men of that fief, who shall be answerable for the revenues to us or to him to whom we have assigned them; and if we give or sell to anyone the wardship of any such land and he causes destruction or waste therein, he shall lose that wardship, and it shall be transferred to two lawful and discreet men of that fief, who shall similarly be answerable to us as is aforesaid.

[5] Moreover, so long as he has the wardship of the land, the guardian shall keep in repair the houses, parks, preserves, ponds, mills and other things pertaining to the land out of the revenues from it; and he shall restore to the heir when he comes of age his land fully stocked with ploughs and the means of husbandry according to what the season of husbandry requires and the revenues of the land can reasonably bear.

[6] Heirs shall be married without disparagement, yet so that before the marriage is

contracted those nearest in blood to the heir shall have notice.

[7] A widow shall have her marriage portion and inheritance forthwith and without difficulty after the death of her husband; nor shall she pay anything to have her dower or her marriage portion or the inheritance which she and her husband held on the day of her husband's death; and she may remain in her husband's house for forty days after his death; within which time her dower shall be assigned to her.

[8] No widow shall be forced to marry so long as she wishes to live without a husband, provided that she gives security not to marry without our consent if she holds of us, or without the consent of her lord of whom she holds, if she holds of another.

[9] Neither we nor our bailiffs will seize for any debt any land or rent, so long as the chattels of the debtor are sufficient to repay the debt; nor will those who have gone surety for the debtor be distrained so long as the principal debtor is himself able to pay the debt; and if the principal debtor fails to pay the debt, having nothing wherewith to pay it, then shall the sureties answer for the debt; and they shall, if they wish, have the lands and rents of the debtor until they are reimbursed for the debt which they have paid for him, unless the principal debtor can show that he has discharged his obligation in the matter to the said sureties.

[10] If anyone who has borrowed from the Jews any sum, great or small, dies before it is repaid, the debt shall not bear interest as long as the heir is under age, of whomsoever he holds; and if the debt falls into our hands, we will not take anything except the principal mentioned in the bond.

[11] And if anyone dies indebted to the Jews, his wife shall have her dower and pay nothing of that debt; and if the dead man leaves children who are under age, they shall be provided with necessaries befitting the holding of the deceased; and the debt shall be paid out of the residue, reserving, however, service due to lords of the land; debts owing to others than Jews shall be dealt with in like manner.

[12] No scutage or aid shall be imposed in our kingdom unless by common counsel of our kingdom except for ransoming our person, for making our eldest son a knight, and for once marrying our eldest daughter; and for these only a reasonable aid shall be levied. Be it done in like manner concerning aids from the city of London.

[13] And the city of London shall have all its ancient liberties and free customs as well by land as by water. Furthermore, we will and grant that all other cities, boroughs, towns, and ports shall have all their liberties and free customs.

[14] And to obtain the common counsel of the kingdom about the assessing of an aid (except in the three cases aforesaid) or of a scutage, we will cause to be summoned the archbishops, bishops, abbots, earls and greater barons, individually by our letters— and, in addition, we will cause to be summoned generally through our sheriffs and bailiffs all those holding of us in chief—for a fixed date, namely, after the expiry of at least forty days, and to a fixed place; and in all letters of such summons we will specify the reason for the summons. And when the summons has thus been made, the business shall proceed on the day appointed, according to the counsel of those present, though not all have come who were summoned.

[15] We will not in future grant any one the right to take an aid from his free men, except for ransoming his person, for making his eldest son a knight and for once marrying his eldest daughter, and for these only reasonable aid shall be levied.

[16] No one shall be compelled to do greater service for a knight's fee or for any other free holding than is due from it.

[17] Common pleas shall not follow our court, but shall be held in some fixed place.

[18] Recognition of *novel disseisin*, of *mort d'ancester*, and of *darrein presentment*, shall not be held elsewhere than in the counties to which they relate, and in this manner— we, or, if we should be out of the realm, our chief justiciar, will send two justices through each county four times a year, who, with four knights of each county chosen by the county, shall hold the said assizes in the county and on the day and in the place of meeting of the county court.

[19] And if the said assizes cannot all be held on the day of the county court, there shall stay behind as many of the knights and freeholders who were present at the county court on that day as are necessary for the

sufficient making of judgments, according to the amount of business to be done.

[20] A free man shall not be amerced for a trivial offence except in accordance with the degree of the offence, and for a grave offence he shall be amerced in accordance with its gravity, yet saving his way of living; and a merchant in the same way, saving his stock-in-trade; and a villein shall be amerced in the same way, saving his means of livelihood—if they have fallen into our mercy; and none of the aforesaid amercements shall be imposed except by the oath of good men of the neighbourhood.

[21] Earls and barons shall not be amerced except by their peers, and only in accordance with the degree of the offence.

[22] No clerk shall be amerced in respect of his lay holding except after the manner of the others aforesaid and not according to the amount of his ecclesiastical benefice.

[23] No vill or individual shall be compelled to make bridges at river banks, except those who from of old are legally bound to do so.

[24] No sheriff, constable, coroners, or others of our bailiffs, shall hold please of our crown.

[25] All counties, hundreds, wapentakes and trithings shall be at the old rents without any additional payment, except our demesne manors.

[26] If anyone holding a lay fief of us dies and our sheriff or bailiff shows our letters patent of summons for a debt that the deceased owed us, it shall be lawful for our sheriff or bailiff to attach and make a list of chattels of the deceased found upon the lay fief to the value of that debt under the supervision of law-worthy men, provided than none of the chattels shall be removed until the debt which is manifest has been paid to us in full; and the residue shall be left to the executors for carrying out the will of the deceased. And if nothing is owing to us from him, all the chattels shall accrue to the deceased, saving to his wife and children their reasonable shares.

[27] If any free man dies without leaving a will, his chattels shall be distributed by his nearest kinsfolk and friends under the supervision of the church, saving to every one the debts which the deceased owed him.

[28] No constable or other bailiff of ours shall take anyone's corn or other chattels unless he pays on the spot in cash for them or can delay payment by arrangement with the seller.

[29] No constable shall compel any knight to give money instead of castle-guard if he is willing to do the guard himself or through another good man, if for some good reason he cannot do it himself; and if we lead or send him on military service, he shall be excused guard in proportion to the time that because of us he has been on service.

[30] No sheriff, or bailiff of ours, or anyone else shall take the horses or carts of any free man for transport work save with the agreement of that freeman.

[31] Neither we nor our bailiffs will take, for castles or other works of ours, timber which is not ours, except with the agreement of him whose timber it is.

[32] We will not hold for more than a year and a day the lands of those convicted of felony, and then the lands shall be handed over to the lords of the fiefs.

[33] Henceforth all fish-weirs shall be cleared completely from the Thames and the Medway and throughout all England, except along the sea coast.

[34] The writ called *Praecipe* shall not in future be issued to anyone in respect of any holding whereby a free man may lose his court.

[35] Let there be one measure for wine throughout our kingdom, and one measure for ale, and one measure for corn, namely "the London quarter"; and one width for cloths whether dyed, russet or halberget, namely two ells within the selvedges. Let it be the same with weights as with measures.

[36] Nothing shall be given or taken in future for the writ of inquisition of life or limbs: instead it shall be granted free of charge and not refused.

[37] If anyone holds of us by fee-farm, by socage, or by burgage, and holds land of another by knight service, we will not, by reason of that fee-farm, socage, or burgage, have the wardship of his heir or of land of his that is of the fief of the other; nor will we have custody of the fee-farm, socage, or burgage, unless such fee-farm owes knight service. We will not have custody of anyone's heir or

land which he holds of another by knight service by reason of any petty serjeanty which he holds of us by the service of rendering to us knives or arrows or the like.

[38] No bailiff shall in future put anyone to trial upon his own bare word, without reliable witnesses produced for this purpose.

[39] No free man shall be arrested or imprisoned or disseised or outlawed or exiled or in any way victimised, neither will we attack him or send anyone to attack him, except by the lawful judgment of his peers or by the law of the land.

[40] To no one will we sell, to no one will we refuse or delay right or justice.

[41] All merchants shall be able to go out of and come into England safely and securely and stay and travel throughout England, as well by land as by water, for buying and selling by the ancient and right customs free from all evil tolls, except in time of war and if they are of the land that is at war with us. And if such are found in our land at the beginning of a war, they shall be attached, without injury to their persons or goods, until we, or our chief justiciar, know how merchants of our land are treated who were found in the land at war with us when war broke out, and if ours are safe there, the others shall be safe in our land.

[42] It shall be lawful in future for anyone, without prejudicing the allegiance due to us, to leave our kingdom and return safely and securely by land and water, save, in the public interest, for a short period in time of war—except for those imprisoned or oulawed in accordance with the law of the kingdom and natives of a land that is at war with us and merchants (who shall be treated as aforesaid).

[43] If anyone who holds of some escheat such as the honour of Wallingford, Nottingham, Boulogne, Lancaster, or of other escheats which are in our hands and are baronies dies, his heir shall give no other relief and do no other service to us than he would have done to the baron if that barony had been in the baron's hands; and we will hold it in the same manner in which the baron held it.

[44] Men who live outside the forest need not henceforth come before our justices of the forest upon a general summons, unless they are impleaded or are sureties for any person or persons who are attached for forest offences.

[45] We will not make justices, constables, sheriffs or bailiffs save of such as know the law of the kingdom and mean to observe it well.

[46] All barons who have founded abbeys for which they have charters of the kings of England or ancient tenure shall have the custody of them during vacancies, as they ought to have.

[47] All forests that have been made forest in our time shall be immediately disafforested; and so be it done with riverbanks that have been made preserves by us in our time.

[48] All evil customs connected with forests and warrens, foresters and warreners, sheriffs and their officials, riverbanks and their wardens shall immediately be inquired into in each county by twelve sworn knights of the same county who are to be chosen by good men of the same county, and within forty days of the completion of the inquiry shall be utterly abolished by them so as never to be restored, provided that we, or our justiciar if we are not in England, know of it first.

[49] We will immediately return all hostages and charters given to us by Englishmen, as security for peace or faithful service.

[50] We will remove completely from office the relations of Gerard de Athée so that in future they shall have no office in England, namely Engelard de Cigogné, Peter and Guy and Andrew de Chanceaux, Guy de Cigogné, Geoffrey de Martigny and his brothers, Philip Marc and his brothers and his nephew Geoffrey, and all their following.

[51] As soon as peace is restored, we will remove from the kingdom all foreign knights, cross-bowmen, serjeants, and mercenaries, who have come with horses and arms to the detriment of the kingdom.

[52] If anyone has been disseised of or kept out of his lands, castles, franchises or his right by us without the legal judgment of his peers, we will immediately restore them to him: and if a dispute arises over this, then let it be decided by the judgment of the twenty-five barons who are mentioned below in the clause for securing the peace: for all the things, however, which anyone has been disseised or kept out of without the lawful judgment of his peers by king Henry, our

father, or by king Richard, our brother, which we have in our hand or are held by others, to whom we are bound to warrant them, we will have the usual period of respite of crusaders, excepting those things about which a plea was started or an inquest made by our command before we took the cross; when however we return from our pilgrimage, or if by any chance we do not go on it, we will at once do full justice therein.

[53] We will have the same respite, and in the same manner, in the doing of justice in the matter of the disafforesting or retaining of the forests which Henry our father or Richard our brother afforested, and in the matter of the wardship of lands which are of the fief of another, wardships of which sort we have hitherto had by reason of a fief which anyone held of us by knight service, and in the matter of abbeys founded on the fief of another, not on a fief of our own, in which the lord of the fief claims he has a right; and when we have returned, or if we do not set out on our pilgrimage, we ill at once do full justice to those who complain of these things.

[54] No one shall be arrested or imprisoned upon the appeal of a woman for the death of anyone except her husband.

[55] All fines made with us unjustly and against the law of the land, and all amercements imposed unjustly and against the law of the land, shall be entirely remitted, or else let them be settled by the judgment of the twenty-five barons who are mentioned below in the clause for securing the peace, or by the judgment of the majority of the same, along with the aforesaid Stephen, archbishop of Canterbury, if he can be present, and such others as he may wish to associate with himself for this purpose, and if he cannot be present the business shall nevertheless proceed without him, provided that if any one or more of the aforesaid twenty-five barons are in a like suit, they shall be removed from the judgment of the case in question, and others chosen, sworn and put in their place by the rest of the same twenty-five for this case only.

[56] If we have disseised or kept out Welshmen from lands or liberties or other things without the legal judgment of their peers in England or in Wales, they shall be immediately restored to them; and if a dispute arises over this, then let it be decided in the March by the judgment of their peers—for holdings in England according to the law of England, for holdings in Wales according to the law of Wales, and for holdings in the March according to the law of the March. Welshmen shall do the same to us and ours.

[57] for all things, however, which any Welshman was disseised of or kept out of without the lawful judgment of his peers by king Henry, our father, or king Richard, our brother, which we have in our hand or which are held by others, to whom we are bound to warrant them, we will have the usual period of respite of crusaders, excepting those things about which a plea was started or an inquest made by our command before we took the cross; when however we return, or if by any chance we do not set out on our pilgrimage, we will at once do full justice to them in accordance with the laws of the Welsh and the foresaid regions.

[58] We will give back at once the son Llywelyn and all the hostages from Wales and the charters that were handed over to us as security for peace.

[59] We will act toward Alexander, king of the Scots, concerning the return of his sisters and hostages and concerning his franchises and his right in the same manner in which we act towards our other barons of England, unless it ought to be otherwise by the charters which we have from William his father, formerly king of the Scots, and this shall be determined by the judgment of his peers in our court.

[60] All these aforesaid customs and liberties which we have granted to be observed in our kingdom as far as it pertains to us towards our men, all of our kingdom, clerks as well as laymen, shall observe as far as it pertains to them towards their men.

[61] Since, moreover, for God and the betterment of our kingdom and for the better allaying of the discord that has arisen between us and our barons we have granted all these things aforesaid, wishing them to enjoy the use of them unimpaired and unshaken for ever, we give and grant them the underwritten security, namely, that the barons shall choose any twenty-five barons of the kingdom they wish, who must with all their might observe, hold and cause to be observed, the

peace and liberties which we have granted and confirmed to them by this present charter of ours, so that if we, or our justiciar, or our bailiffs or any one of our servants offend in any way against anyone or transgress any of the articles of the peace or the security and the offence be notified to four of the aforesaid twenty-five barons, those four barons shall come to us, or to our justiciar if we are out of the kingdom, and, laying the transgression before us, shall petition us to have that transgression corrected without delay. And if we do not correct the transgression, or if we are out of the kingdom, if our justiciar does not correct it, within forty days, reckoning from the time it was brought to our notice or to that of our justiciar if we were out of the kingdom, the aforesaid four barons shall refer that case to the rest of the twenty-five barons and those twenty-five barons together with the community of the whole land shall distrain and distress us in every way they can, namely, by seizing castles, lands, possessions, and in such other ways as they can saving our person and the persons of our queen and our children, until, in their opinion amends have been made, and when amends have been made, they shall obey us as they did before. And let anyone in the land who wishes take an oath to obey the orders of the said twenty-five barons for the execution of all the aforesaid matters, and with them to distress us as much as he can, and we publicly and freely give anyone leave to take the oath who wishes to take it and we will never prohibit anyone from taking it. Indeed, all those in the land who are unwilling of themselves and of their own accord to take an oath to the twenty-five barons to help them to distrain and distress us, we will make them take the oath as aforesaid at our command. And if any of the twenty-five barons dies or leaves the country or is in any other way prevented from carrying out the things aforesaid, the rest of the aforesaid twenty-five barons shall choose as they think fit another one in his place, and he shall take the oath like the rest. In all matters the execution of which is committed to these twenty-five barons, if it should happen that these twenty-five are present yet disagree among themselves about anything, or if some of those summoned will not or cannot be present, that shall be held as fixed and established which the majority of those present ordained or commanded, exactly as if all the twenty-five had consented to it; and the said twenty-five shall swear that they will faithfully observe all the things aforesaid and will do all they can to get them observed. And we will procure nothing from anyone, either personally or through anyone else, whereby any of these concessions and liberties might be revoked or diminished; and if any such thing is procured, let it be void and null, and we will never use it either personally or through another.

[62] And we have fully remitted and pardoned to everyone all the ill-will, indignation and rancour that have arisen between us and our men, clergy and laity, from the time of the quarrel. Furthermore, we have fully remitted to all, clergy and laity, and as far as pertains to us have completely forgiven, all trespasses occasioned by the same quarrel between Easter in the sixteenth year of our reign and the restoration of peace. And, besides, we have caused to be made for them letters testimonial patent of the lord Stephen archbishop of Canterbury, of the lord Henry archbishop of Dublin and of the aforementioned bishops and of master Pandulf about this security and the aforementioned concessions.

[63] Wherefore we wish and firmly enjoin that the English church shall be free, and that the men in our kingdom shall have and hold all the aforesaid liberties, rights and concessions well and peacefully, freely and quietly, fully and completely, for themselves and their heirs from us and our heirs, in all matters and in all places for ever, as is aforesaid. An oath, moreover, has been taken, as well on our part as on the part of the barons, that all these things aforesaid shall be observed in good faith and without evil disposition. Witness the above-mentioned and many others. Given by our hand in the meadow which is called Runnymede between Windsor and Staines on the fifteenth day of June, in the seventeenth year of our reign.

Bill of Rights [1689]

An Act Declaring the Rights and Liberties of the Subject and Settling the Succession of the Crown

Whereas the Lords Spiritual and Temporal and Commons assembled at Westminster, lawfully, fully and freely representing all the estates of the people of this realm, did upon the thirteenth day of February in the year of our Lord one thousand six hundred eighty-eight present unto their Majesties, then called and known by the names and style of William and Mary, prince and princess of Orange, being present in their proper persons, a certain declaration in writing made by the said Lords and Commons in the words following, viz.:

Whereas the late King James the Second, by the assistance of divers evil counsellors, judges and ministers employed by him, did endeavour to subvert and extirpate the Protestant religion and the laws and liberties of this kingdom;

By assuming and exercising a power of dispensing with and suspending of laws and the execution of laws without consent of Parliament;

By committing and prosecuting divers worthy prelates for humbly petitioning to be excused from concurring to the said assumed power;

By issuing and causing to be executed a commission under the great seal for erecting a court called the Court of Commissioners for Ecclesiastical Causes;

By levying money for and to the use of the Crown by pretence of prerogative for other time and in other manner than the same was granted by Parliament;

By raising and keeping a standing army within this kingdom in time of peace without consent of Parliament, and quartering soldiers contrary to law;

By causing several good subjects being Protestants to be disarmed at the same time when papists were both armed and employed contrary to law;

By violating the freedom of election of members to serve in Parliament;

By prosecutions in the Court of King's Bench for matters and causes cognizable only in Parliament, and by divers other arbitrary and illegal courses;

And whereas of late years partial corrupt and unqualified persons have been returned and served on juries in trials, and particularly divers jurors in trials for high treason which were not freeholders;

And excessive bail hath been required of persons committed in criminal cases to elude the benefit of the laws made for the liberty of the subjects;

And excessive fines have been imposed;

And illegal and cruel punishments inflicted;

And several grants and promises made of fines and forfeitures before any conviction or judgment against the persons upon whom the same were to be levied;

All which are utterly and directly contrary to the known laws and statutes and freedom of this realm;

And whereas the said late King James the Second having abdicated the government and the throne being thereby vacant, his Highness the prince of Orange (whom it hath pleased Almighty God to make the glorious instrument of delivering this kingdom from popery and arbitrary power) did (by the advice of the Lords Spiritual and Temporal and divers principal persons of the Commons) cause letters to be written to the Lords Spiritual and Temporal being Protestants, and other letters to the several counties, cities, universities, boroughs and cinque ports, for the choosing of such persons to represent them as were of right to be sent to Parliament, to meet and sit at Westminster upon the two and twentieth day of January in this year one thousand six hundred eighty and eight, in order to such an establishment as that their religion, laws and liberties might not again be in danger of being subverted, upon which letters elections having been accordingly made;

And thereupon the said Lords Spiritual and Temporal and Commons, pursuant to their respective letters and elections, being now assembled in a full and free representative of this nation, taking into their most serious consideration the best means for attaining the ends aforesaid, do in the first place (as their ancestors in like case have usually done) for the vindicating and asserting their ancient rights and liberties declare

That the pretended power of suspending of laws or the execution of laws by regal authority without consent of Parliament is illegal;

That the pretended power of dispensing with laws or the execution of laws by regal authority, as it hath been assumed and exercised of late, is illegal;

That the commission for erecting the late Court of Commissioners for Ecclesiastical Causes, and all other commissions and courts of like nature, are illegal and pernicious;

That levying money for or to the use of the Crown by pretence of prerogative, without grant of Parliament, for longer time, or in other manner than the same is or shall be granted, is illegal;

That it is the right of the subjects to petition the king, and all commitments and prosecutions for such petitioning are illegal;

That the raising or keeping a standing army within the kingdom in time of peace, unless it be with consent of Parliament, is against law;

That the subjects which are Protestants may have arms for their defence suitable to their conditions and as allowed by law;

That election of members of Parliament ought to be free;

That the freedom of speech and debates or proceedings in Parliament ought not to be impeached or questioned in any court or place out of Parliament;

That excessive bail ought not to be required, nor excessive fines imposed, nor cruel and unusual punishments inflicted;

That jurors ought to be duly impanelled and returned, and jurors which pass upon men in trials for high treason ought to be freeholders;

That all grants and promises of fines and forfeitures of particular persons before conviction are illegal and void;

And that for redress of all grievances, and for the amending, strengthening and preserving of the laws, Parliaments ought to be held frequently.

And they do claim, demand and insist upon all and singular the premises as their undoubted rights and liberties, and that no declarations, judgments, doings or proceedings to the prejudice of the people in any of the said premises ought in any wise to be drawn hereafter into consequence or example; to which demand of their rights they are particularly encouraged by the declaration of his Highness the prince of Orange as being the only means for obtaining a full redress and remedy therein. Having therefore an entire confidence that his said Highness the prince of Orange will perfect the deliverance so far advanced by him, and will still preserve them from the violation of their rights which they have here asserted, and from all other attempts upon their religion, rights and liberties, the said Lords Spiritual and Temporal and Commons assembled at Westminster do resolve that William and Mary, prince and princess of Orange, be and be declared king and queen of England, France and Ireland and the dominions thereunto belonging, to hold the crown and loyal dignity of the said kingdoms and dominions to them, the said prince and princess, during their lives and the life of the survivor of them, and that the sole and full exercise of the legal power be only in and executed by the said prince of Orange in the names of the said prince and princess during their joint lives, and after their deceases the said crown and loyal dignity of the said kingdoms and dominions to be to the heirs of the body of the said princess, and for default of such issue to the Princess Anne of Denmark and the heirs of the body of the said prince of Orange. And the Lords Spiritual and Temporal and Commons do pray the said prince and princess to accept the same accordingly.

And that the oaths hereafter mentioned be taken by all persons of whom the oaths of allegiance and supremacy might be required by law, instead of them; and that the said oaths of allegiance and supremacy be abrogated.

I, A.B., do sincerely promise and swear that I will be faithful and bear true allegiance to their Majesties King William and Queen Mary. So help me God.

I, A.B., do swear that I do from my heart abhor, detest and abjure as impious and heretical this damnable doctrine and position, that princes excommunicated or deprived by the Pope or any authority of the see of Rome may be deposed or murdered by their subjects or any other whatsoever. And I do declare that no foreign prince, person, prelate, state or potentate hath or ought to have any jurisdiction, power, superiority, pre-eminence or authority, ecclesiastical or spiritual, within this realm. So help me God.

Upon which their said Majesties did

accept the crown and royal dignity of the kingdoms of England, France and Ireland, and the dominions thereunto belonging, according to the resolution and desire of the said Lords and Commons contained in the said declaration. And thereupon their Majesties were pleased that the said Lords Spiritual and Temporal and Commons, being the two Houses of Parliament, should continue to sit, and with their Majesties' royal concurrence make effectual provision for the settlement of the religion, laws and liberties of this kingdom, so that the same for the future might not be in danger again of being subverted, to which the said Lords Spiritual and Temporal and Commons did agree, and proceed to act accordingly. Now in pursuance of the premises the said Lords Spiritual and Temporal and Commons in Parliament assembled for the ratifying, confirming and establishing the said declaration and the articles, clauses, matters and things therein contained by the force of a law made in due form by authority of Parliament, do pray that it may be declared and enacted that all and singular the rights and liberties asserted and claimed in the said declaration are the true, ancient and indubitable rights and liberties of the people of this kingdom, and so shall be esteemed, allowed, adjudged, deemed and taken to be; and that all and every the particulars aforesaid shall be firmly and strictly holden and observed as they are expressed in the said declaration, and all officers and ministers whatsoever shall serve their Majesties and their successors according to the same in all times to come. And the said Lords Spiritual and Temporal and Commons, seriously considering how it hath pleased Almighty God in his marvellous providence and merciful goodness to this nation to provide and preserve their said Majesties' royal persons most happily to reign over us upon the throne of their ancestors, for which they render unto him from the bottom of their hearts their humblest thanks and praises, do truly, firmly, assuredly and in the sincerity of their hearts think, and do hereby recognize, acknowledge and declare, that King James the Second having abdicated the government, and their Majesties having accepted the crown and royal dignity as aforesaid, their said Majesties did become, were, are and of right ought to be by the laws of this realm our sovereign liege lord and lady, king and queen of England, France and Ireland and the dominions thereunto belonging, in and to whose princely persons the royal state, crown and dignity of the said realms with all honours, styles, titles, regalities, prerogatives, powers, jurisdictions and authorities to the same belonging and appertaining are most fully, rightfully and entirely invested and incorporated, united and annexed. And for preventing all questions and divisions in this realm by reason of any pretended titles to the crown, and for preserving a certainty in the succession thereof, in and upon which the unity, peace, tranquillity and safety of this nation doth under God wholly consist and depend, the said Lords Spiritual and Temporal and Commons do beseech their Majesties that it may be enacted, established and declared, that the crown and regal government of the said kingdoms and dominions, with all and singular the premises thereunto belonging and appertaining, shall be and continue to their said Majesties and the survivor of them during their lives and the life of the survivor of them, and that the entire, perfect and full exercise of the regal power and government be only in and executed by his Majesty in the names of both their Majesties during their joint lives; and after their deceases the said crown and premises shall be and remain to the heirs of the body of her Majesty, and for default of such issue to her Royal Highness the Princess Anne of Denmark and the heirs of her body, and for default of such issue to the heirs of the body of his said Majesty; and thereunto the said Lords Spiritual and Temporal and Commons do in the name of all the people aforesaid most humbly and faithfully submit themselves, their heirs and posterities for ever, and do faithfully promise that they will stand to, maintain and defend their said Majesties, and also the limitation and succession of the crown herein specified and contained, to the utmost of their powers with their lives and estates against all persons whatsoever that shall attempt anything to the contrary. And whereas it hath been found by experience that it is inconsistent with the safety and welfare of this Protestant kingdom to be governed by a popish prince, or by any king or queen marrying a papist, the said Lords Spiritual and Temporal and Commons do further pray that it may be enacted, that all and every person and persons that is, are or shall be reconciled to or shall hold communion with the see or Church of Rome, or shall profess the popish religion, or shall marry a papist, shall be excluded and be for ever incapable to inherit, possess or enjoy the crown and government of this realm and Ireland and the dominions there unto belonging or any part of the same, or to have, use or exercise any regal power, authority or jurisdiction within the same; and in all and every such case or cases the people of these realms shall be and are hereby absolved of their allegiance; and the said crown and government shall from time to time descend to and be enjoyed by such person or persons being Protestants as should have inherited and enjoyed the same in case the said person or persons so reconciled, holding communion or professing or marrying as aforesaid were naturally dead; and that every king and queen of this realm who at any time hereafter shall come to and succeed in the imperial crown of this kingdom shall on the first day of the meeting of the first Parliament next after his or her coming to the crown, sitting in his or her throne in the House of Peers in the presence of the Lords and Commons therein assembled, or at his or her coronation before such person or persons who shall administer the coronation oath to him or her at the time of his or her taking the said oath (which shall first happen), make, subscribe and audibly repeat the declaration mentioned in the statute made in the thirtieth year of the reign of King Charles the Second entituled, *An Act for the more effectual preserving the king's person and government by disabling papists from sitting in either House of Parliament.* But if it shall happen that such king or queen upon his or her succession to the crown of this realm shall be under the age of twelve years, then every such king or queen shall make, subscribe and audibly repeat the said declaration at his or her coronation or the first day of the meeting of the first Parliament as aforesaid which shall first happen after such king or queen shall have attained the said age of twelve years. All which their Majesties are contented and pleased shall be declared, enacted and established by authority of this present Parliament, and shall stand, remain and be the law of this realm for ever; and the same are by their said Majesties, by and with the advice and consent of the Lords Spiritual and Temporal and Commons in Parliament assembled and by the authority of the same, declared, enacted and established accordingly.

II. And be it further declared and enacted by the authority aforesaid, that from and after this present session of Parliament no dispensation by *non obstante* of or to any statute or any part thereof shall be allowed, but that the same shall be held void and of no effect, except a dispensation be allowed of in such statute, and except in such cases as shall be specially provided for by one or more bill or bills to be passed during this present session of Parliament.

III. Provided that no charter or grant or pardon granted before the three and twentieth day of October in the year of our Lord one thousand six hundred eighty-nine shall be any ways impeached or invalidated by this Act, but that the same shall be and remain of the same force and effect in law and no other than as if this Act had never been made.

The Mayflower Compact

In ye name of God Amen. We whose names are underwritten, the loyall subjects of our dread soveraigne Lord King James, by ye grace of God, of Great Britaine, France, & Ireland king, defender of ye faith, & c. Haveing undertaken, for ye glorie of God, and advancemente of ye Christian faith and honour of our king & countrie, a voyage to plant ye first colonie in ye Northerne parts of Virginia, doe by these presents solemnly & mutualy in ye presence of God, and one of another, covenant, & combine ourselves togeather into a Civill body politick; for our better ordering, & preservation & furtherance of ye ends aforesaid; and by vertue hereof to enacte, constitute, and frame such just & equall Lawes, ordinances, Acts, constitutions, & offices, from time to time, as shall be thought most meete & convenient for ye generall good of ye colonie: unto which we promise all due submission and obedience. In witnes whereof we have hereunder subscribed our names at Cap-Codd ye -11- of November, in ye year of ye raigne of our soveraigne Lord King James of England, France, & Ireland ye eighteenth, and of Scotland ye fiftie fourth. Ano Dom. 1620.

JOHN CARVER
WILLIAM BRADFORD
EDWARD WINSLOW
WILLIAM BREWSTER
JOSES FLETCHER
JOHN GOODMAN
SAMUEL FULLER
CHRISTOPHER MARTIN
WILLIAM MULLINS
WILLIAM WHITE
RICHARD WARREN
JOHN HOWLAND
STEPHEN HOPKINS
DIGERY PRIEST
ISAAC ALLERTON
MILES STANDISH
JOHN ALDEN
JOHN TURNER
THOMAS WILLIAMS
GILBERT WINSLOW
EDMUND MARGESSON

PETER BROWN
RICHARD BITTERIDGE
GEORGE SOULE
EDWARD TILLY
JOHN TILLY
FRANCIS COOKE
THOMAS ROGERS
FRANCIS EATON
JAMES CHILTON
JOHN CRAXTON
JOHN BILLINGTON
THOMAS TINKER
JOHN RIDGATE
EDWARD FULLER
RICHARD CLARK
RICHARD GARDINER
JOHN ALLERTON
THOMAS ENGLISH
EDWARD DOTEN
EDWARD LIESTER

GLOSSARY

FOR THE CONSTITUTION AND LANDMARK CASES

a

abolition: the act of doing away with totally; putting an end to

abridge: to limit; to cut short

absolutist view of free speech: a judicial view that the First Amendment means that speakers cannot ever be punished for what they say but that they may be punished for the place, time, or way in which they say it

affirmative action policy: a government policy that encourages or requires employers and educators to actively seek and hire minority applicants for jobs or other positions

appeal: to take a lower court's decision to a higher court

appellate: a court that has the power to hear appeals from lower courts and to reverse lower court decisions

apportion: to divide and distribute according to plan

appropriation: an amount of money set aside for a special purpose

b

bail: the money posted with the court that allows a person accused of a crime to be released from jail and acts as a guarantee that the person will appear in court for trial

balancing view of free speech: a judicial view that speech rights can be balanced against other government goals

bill: a proposed law

bill of attainder: a legislative measure that condemns and punishes a person without benefit of a jury trial

c

charter: a contract or grant

commerce: trade; business

compensation: salary

concurrence: agreement

constitution: the basic law of a nation or state

convene: call together

d

deprive: to deny; to take something away from

dissent: to differ in opinion

docket: a list of cases to be tried by a court of law

domestic tranquility: establishment of order within the country

due process of law: fair and legal proceedings

duty: a tax on imported or exported goods

e

elector: voter who actually elects the president and vice president

emancipation: freedom; the act of freeing from bondage

emolument: payment; salary

enumerated power: power that is listed in the Constitution

enumeration: counting; census

evict: to expel a tenant from land or a building

excise: a tax on a product manufactured within the country

execute: to carry out

executive privilege: a right of the president to keep presidential matters confidential

expedient: suitable; advisable

ex post facto law: a law that punishes a person for doing something before the law making it illegal was passed

f

federalism: a system of government whereby power is divided among levels of government

felony: a serious crime

fundamental liberties view: a judicial view that what is necessary for justice may go beyond the promises made in the first eight amendments to the Bill of Rights

g

grand jury: a group of people who decide whether or not someone should be formally accused of a crime

h

habeas corpus: a legal order to bring a person before a court in order to determine whether the person has been lawfully imprisoned

i

illiterate: unable to read or write

immunity: protection

impartial: not biased or prejudiced

impeachment: a charge of wrongdoing

implied power: a power that is understood because it is necessary to help carry out an enumerated power

impost: a tax on imported goods

incorporation view: a judicial view that the 14th Amendment applies the first eight amendments in the Bill of Rights to state court procedures

indictment: formal accusation

infringe: to violate or go beyond the limits

inherent power: power assumed by a president that the Constitution does not specify

insurrection: an act of open rebellion against an established government

j

jeopardy: danger or loss; the peril a defendant faces when put on trial for a crime

judicial review: the power of the Supreme Court to decide if laws passed by Congress are constitutional

jurisdiction: the right to interpret and apply the law

jury: a group of 12 people who determine guilt or innocence at criminal and civil trials

l

laissez-faire: the economic policy maintaining that there should be very little government involvement with the economy

letter of marque and reprisal: license once used to allow a privately owned ship to capture an enemy ship

m

militia: citizen-soldiers who are not in the regular army; today it refers to the National Guard units of the states

misdemeanor: a less serious crime than a felony, such as theft of a small amount of money

o

ordain: order; decree

overt: open to view; observable

p

paternalism: the theory maintaining that people should be kept from hurting themselves; the theory that a country or group of people should be treated in a manner suggestive of a father handling his children

petition: a formal request

posterity: future generations

precedent: a decision by a court of law that serves as an example for deciding future similar cases

president elect: the person who has been elected president but who has not yet taken office

pro tempore: for the time being

prohibition: an order to stop; a law that makes something illegal

q

quarter: lodge; house

quorum: the number of persons needed to be present to conduct business

quota system: a rule stating that certain percentages of jobs, promotions, or other types of selections must be given to members of minority groups

r

radicalism: supporting of extreme measures for change in political, social, or economic institutions

ratification: official approval

redress: to correct a wrong

repeal: to officially withdraw or cancel

reprieve: the temporary suspension of a sentence

requisite: essential; necessary

revenue: money; income

rule of naturalization: the process by which foreign-born people can become citizens of the United States

s

sect: a relatively small group having the same philosophical beliefs

segregation: practice of separating groups of people

suffrage: right of voting

t

tender: money offered in payment of a debt

treason: betrayal of one's country

tribunal: court of justice

u

unanimous: in complete agreement; of one mind and opinion

undocumented aliens: foreigners who do not have papers showing that they have permission to be in the country

v

vested: held or established

w

warrant: judicial order authorizing arrest, search, or seizure

welfare: health, happiness, general well-being

writ: a legal document asking someone to perform or refrain from an act